Aliens, Angels, and Gods:
Encoding the DNA of Man

Emanuel Rapha

Aliens, Angels, and Gods: Encoding the DNA of Man

Emanuel Rapha

Copyright © 2013

All rights reserved.

Fifth Estate Publishers,

First Printing 2013

Cover art by An Quigley

Printed on acid-free paper

Library of Congress Control No: 2013933615

ISBN: 9781936533336

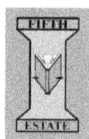

Fifth Estate
Copyright © 2013

DEDICATION

Seekers, mystics, and those who have the courage to look beyond the walls of society and religion, this book is for you.

CONTENTS

Introduction

Somewhere in our antediluvian past mankind both
technologically and socially surged forward in a single leap, from
being hunter-gatherers to city dwellers and inventors, we
intellectually bloomed in a second of historical time. For millions
of years we, as a species, saw little change, but around the time
primitive men began drawing pictures in caves depicting aliens,
flying machines, and spacecraft suddenly everything changed and
man began to invent, create, build, and imagine a future.
Synchronicity of these events cannot go unnoticed.

The development of the wheel, the building of ornate astrological
temples, the invention of writing, math, and all the technology
that would lead to the modern age took place in seemingly a blink
of an eye. For millions of years humanoids struggled to survive
with little discernible advancement in their technology or skills,
then overnight mankind began to develop at an amazing rate. For
10 million years we lived as animals lived, as cave dwellers,
hunting and gathering when we could, where we could. Then
they came, and everything changed. We began to read and write.
We began living in cities. We began wild adventures of creativity.
We built pyramids. We learned about the stars. We could predict
solar and lunar events.

We became brighter, more intelligent, certainly more creative and inventive. To what do we owe this quantum leap in our development? The mere act of discovering or learning does not answer the question fully. We were thinking differently, deeper, more logically. We were being changed, altered, our DNA being manipulated. We were being made better. But for what purpose and toward what end was mankind being changed?

We will examine various ancient sources in order to piece together the puzzle of the creation and evolution of mankind. From the concepts of gods, angels and aliens to the realization we ourselves could be a divine experiment, we will weave together a story based on documents older than Christianity itself showing a path of creation, experimentation, observation, and documentation on the part of beings we call Angels aliens and gods.

In The Beginning There Were Gods

In the beginning the gods created the heavens and the earth. So says the literal translation of Genesis 1:1.

"In the beginning Elohim created the heavens and the earth." The word for Gods in the Old Testament is Elohim.

When the letters IM appear on the end of a Hebrew noun it means the word is masculine - plural. Elohim is a masculine - plural noun. Cherubim are many cherubs. Seraphim are many seraphs. Elohim are many Els or gods. Is this a trace left behind by the Holy Bible, pointing to the original creation of man by many gods or a race of Gods? Were these gods divine beings, angels or aliens? Both Genesis 1:1, Deut 32, and Psalms 82 tell us there was more than one being defined as a god.

Christian scholars agree with the fact the word Elohim is plural, but argue that the plurality is explained away by what they call the "royal we", as when a king or queen refers to his or her self in the plural. Literalists cease taking the Bible literally when it comes to translating the word Elohim as "gods". Scholars point out that the plural noun should be translated in the singular when put alongside a singular verb, yet this rule is only applied strictly to Genesis 1:1 and is not followed in the same book in other identical occurrences such as in Genesis 20:13, Gen 35:7, 2 Sam 7:23, and Psalms 58. In these writings the word Elohim is followed by a plural verb but it still translated "God."

If God is singular the word used should be "Eloah." The fact that the word Eloah is used approximately 250 times in the Bible shows the choice of the usage was deliberate in Genesis 1:1 and other places.

When the writers of the Old Testament wished to refer to multiple gods of other religions they used Elohim to denote plural gods.

The writers of The Old Testament referred to multiple Gods 'Elohim' no less than 2,500 times. This shows a decision and choice of usage.

So let's not forget, the word for multiple Gods appears ten times more in the Old Testament than description of a singular entity. There are also other clear references to multiple Gods in the scriptures, such as Genesis 1:26, which states:

"Let us make man in our image".
(Later we shall discuss this statement as evidence of cloning or DNA engineering which yielded a human race resembling their creators.)

Christian scholars attempt to discount this text by claiming God is part of a trinity, but the concept of the trinity was invented in the time of Constantine. Jews had no such doctrine or belief. Further, their belief is summed up as "Hear o Israel, they Lord thy God is One. But the word for Lord (Yahweh) and the word for god, (El), is different. This Trinitarian concept does not hold true constantly when we examine such passages as "Hear O Israel! The Lord is our God, the Lord is one!" (Deuteronomy 6:4).

Thus, somewhere between Genesis:
"Behold, the man has become like one of US" (Gen 3:22)
and Deuteronomy there was a shift from the concept of gods to a single god. The singular god of the Israelites was known as Yahweh.

It appears there was an assembly of gods and the commander of these creatures divided up the peoples of the earth, giving each god a portion and people to oversee. Yahweh received Israel to tend.

This is a very important concept and needs repeating. There were multiple gods. It is possible, as we will see later, that we were created by a team of these beings, but at one time in the past, according to the book of Genesis, various areas and peoples were given to certain gods to tend and husband as a farmer would watch over his sheep as they graze. Israel was handed over to the god Yahweh.

In the earliest stages of the religion of the Jews, Yahweh appears to be simply one of these seventy children, each of whom was the patron deity of the seventy nations. We see this idea of city-states having patron gods brought into the ancient Greek religions as well. The idea also appears in the Dead Sea Scrolls reading and the Septuagint translation of Deuteronomy 32:8.

Deuteronomy 32:8-9
Douay-Rheims 1899 American Edition (DRA)
8) When the Most High divided the nations: when he separated the sons of Adam, he appointed the bounds of people according to the number of the children of Israel
9) And his people Jacob became the portion of the Lord (Yahweh), Israel was the line of his inheritance.

The people of the region worshiped a god called, "El." Ugaritic polytheism consists of a divine council or assembly. The divine family, made up of the chief god, his wife, and their offspring, populates this assembly. The chief god, El, and his wife, Ashtoreth, are said to have produced seventy divine children, some of whose names may be familiar, as they include Baal, Astarte, Anat, Resheph, the sun-goddess Shapshu, and the moon-god Yerak. Some sources also list the name, Yah, or Yahweh. These children came to be called, "the stars of El." (See Job 38:7) Below the divine counsel are the helpers of the divine household. Kothar wa-Hasis was the head of these helpers. Some scholars believe that the servants or helpers of the divine household came to be known as the entities the Bible calls "angels." The word for angel means messenger, and these helpers were in fact, messenger-gods. Ashtoreth would become Asherah in the Israelite's worship.

In fact, ancient gods were named within the league of angels from the beginning. Those great god-kings and demigods of old are among the first angels who fell from the grace of their commander, El.

As the patriarch, El, had divided the land, each member of the divine family received a nation of his own: Israel is the portion of Yahweh. The statement, "according to the number of the children of Israel" is thought to include the seventy children.

Psalm 82 also presents the god, El, presiding over a divine assembly at which Yahweh stands up and makes his accusation against the other gods.

Psalm 82
Amplified Bible (AMP)
A Psalm of Asaph.

1) *GOD (El) stands in the assembly [of the representatives] of God; in the midst of the magistrates or judges He gives judgment [as] among the gods.*

2) *How long will you [magistrates or judges] judge unjustly and show partiality to the wicked? Selah [pause, and calmly think of that]!*

3) *Do justice to the weak (poor) and fatherless; maintain the rights of the afflicted and needy.*

4) *Deliver the poor and needy; rescue them out of the hand of the wicked.*

5) *[The magistrates and judges] know not, neither will they understand; they walk on in the darkness [of complacent satisfaction]; all the foundations of the earth [the fundamental principles upon which rests the administration of justice] are shaking.*

6) *I said, You are gods [since you judge on My behalf, as My representatives]; indeed, all of you are children of the Most High.*

7) *But you shall die as men and fall as one of the princes.*

8) *Arise, O God, judge the earth! For to You belong all the nations.*

If the idea of multiple deities within a monotheistic religion such as Christianity is unsettling to you, look closer at the King James Bible rendering of the verses.

God standeth in the Congregation of God (El)
In the midst of gods (elohim) He judgeth.
All the foundations of the earth are moved.
I said: Ye are gods,
And all of you sons of the Most High (Elyon)
Nevertheles ye shall die like men,
And fall like one of the princes (sarim)
Psalm 82:1, 5-7

As this verse implies, there seem to be multiple gods produced or commanded by a single superior creative entity, since they are called sons, and like any family – some offspring are simply evil. These are warned that due to their actions, even though they are gods, they will fall and die like any mortal prince.

Some sources, including the Masoretic Text; Dead Sea Scrolls (see also Septuagint) renders "children of Israel" instead of "sons of God." The meaning of the name "Israel" is "Who prevails with God" a name showing conflict.

It is not clear whether the people were told El had a wife or if Ashtoreth was simply a female in the group of a mostly male group.

We know from the old records there were at least 200 angels assigned the task of monitoring humans. It was there two-hundred angels, gods, or aliens who came down to earth at the same time and bred with the women. El decided exiling them to the land they had chosen to invade was their punishment. Some sources say he did not allow their return, one source indicates only much, much later did the exiles return, and only then to be held as prisoners within the house of El. After this event there were at least 70 trusted angels left. These 70 would each receive a parcel to protect and command, keeping it free of other angelic invaders. They were also to rule as gods.

Here is a stylized description of the place and power of the watchers taken from the Third Book of Enoch (published by Fifth Estate).

CHAPTER 27

RADWERIEL, the keeper of the Book of Records.

Rabbi Ishmael said: Metatron, the Angel of YHWH, the Prince of the Presence, said to me: (1) Above the Seraphim there is one prince, exalted above all princes. He is more wonderful than all the servants. His name is RADWERIEL YHWH who is assigned to rule over the treasuries of the books.

Radweriel is appointed over the treasury of book of records or remembrances. (See Mal.3:16). He is an angelic scribe, fluent in reading and writing. He reads the records in the Beth Din, (house/court) of justice. This is another name for the Sanhedrin.

(2) He couriers the Case of Writings, which has the Books of Records in it, and he brings it to the Holy One, blessed be He. And he breaks the seals of the case, opens it, and takes out the books and delivers them before the Holy One, blessed be He. And the Holy One, blessed be He, receives them out of his hand and gives them to the Scribes to see so they may read them in the Great Beth (house) Din in the height of Araboth (highest heaven) of Raqia (heaven), before the household of heaven...

CHAPTER 28

The 'Irin and Qaddishin (Watchers and Holy Ones)

Rabbi Ishmael said: Metatron, the Angel, the Prince of the Presence, said to me: (1) Above all these there are four great princes. Their names are Irin and Qaddishin. (The Watchers and the Holy Ones.) They are highly honored, revered, loved, wonderfully glorious, and greater than any of the heavenly children. There is none like them among all the princes of heaven (sky). There are none equal to them among any Servants. Each one is equal to all the rest of the heavenly servants put together. (2) And their dwelling is near the Throne of Glory and their standing place near the Holy One, blessed be He. The brightness of their dwelling is a reflection from the brightness from the Throne of Glory. Their face is magnificent and is a reflection of the magnificence of Shekina. (3) They are elevated by the glory of the Divince Majesty (Gebura) and praised by (through) the praise of Shekina. (4) And not only that, but the Holy One, blessed be He, does nothing in his world without first consulting them. Only after He consults them does He perform it. As it is written (Dan. 4: 17): "The sentence is by the decree of the Irin and the demand by the word of the Qaddishin." (5) The Irin are two (twins) and the Qaddishin are two (twins). In what fashions standing before the Holy One, blessed be He? We should understood, that one Ir is standing on one side and the other 'Ir on the other side. Also, one Qaddish is standing on one side and the other on the other side. (6) And they exalt the humble forever, and they humble and bring to the ground those that are proud. They exalt to the heights those that are humble. (7) And every day, as the Holy One, blessed be

He, is sitting upon the Throne of Judgment and judges the entire world, and the Books of the Living and the Books of the Dead are opened in front of Him all the children of heaven are standing before Him in fear and dread. They are in awe and they shake. When the Holy One, blessed be He, is sitting on the Throne of Judgment to execute His judgment , His garment is white as snow, the hair on His head is like pure wool and His entire cloak is shining with light. He is covered with righteousness all over, like He is wearing a coat of mail. (8) And those Irin and Qaddishin (Watchers and Holy Ones) are standing before Him like court officers before the judge. And constantly they begin and argue a case and close the case that comes before the Holy One, blessed be He, in judgment, according for it is written (Dan. 4. 17): "The sentence is by the decree of the 'Irin and the demand by the word of Qaddishin."

This section explains the function of the Irin and Qaddishin. They are two pairs of angels forming the apex of angelic power. They are the holy councilors and they have authority over all things terrestrial. They are judge and executioner. Another tradition has the Irin and Qaddishin as two classes of angels but many in number. Yet, they seem to come in sets of two each, like twins. Again, this may represent the balance of mercy and justice always sought in heaven. In the case of the Irin and Qaddishin, the ending letters of IN indicate a plural noun.

(9) Some of them argue the case and others pass the sentence in the Great Beth Din (Great House of the Sanhedrin) in Araboth (the

highest heaven). Some of them make requests in the presence of the Divine Majesty and some close the cases before the Most High. Others finish by going down and confirming the judgement and executing the sentences on earth below. According for it is written (Dan. 4. 13, 14): "Behold an Ir and a Qaddish came down from heaven and cried aloud and said , "Chop down the tree, and cut off his branches, shake off his leaves, and scatter his fruit: let the beasts escape from under it, and the fowls from his branches." (10) Why are they called Irin and Qaddishin (Watchers and Holy Ones)? Because they sanctify the body and the spirit with beatings with fire on the third day of the judgment, for it is written (Hos. 6: 2): "After two days will he revive us: on the third he will raise us up, and we shall live before him."

Irin and Qaddishin or ministering spirits receive men from the angel of death. They judge him with angels arguing for him. This takes two days. On the third day they pass judgment. The sentence is based on the man's character and how closely he followed the Torah. They beat them accordingly.

In the 18th Chapter of the Second Book of Enoch we see the punishment of the Watchers.

Chapter 18:1 The men took me to the fifth heaven and placed me, and there I saw many and countless soldiers, called Grigori (Watchers), of human appearance, and their size (was) greater than that of great giants and their faces withered, and the silence of their mouths perpetual, and their was no service on the fifth heaven, and I said to the men who were with me:

(Note: The Greek transliteration egegoroi are the Watchers; a group of fallen angels who mated with mortal women and produced the Nephilim mentioned in the books of Jubilees, 1Enoch, and Genesis 6:4.)

2 Why are they so very withered and their faces melancholy, and their mouths silent, and why is there no service in this heaven? 3 And they said to me: These are the Grigori, who with their prince Satanail (Satan) rejected the Lord of Light. After them are those who are held in great darkness in the second heaven, and three of them went down on to earth from the Lord's throne, to the place Ermon, and broke through their vows on the shoulder of the hill Ermon and saw the daughters of men how good they are, and took to themselves wives, and fouled the earth with their deeds, who broke the law and mixing (with the women), giants are born and amazingly large men with great hatred.

(Note: The Hill of Ermon could be Mount Hermon, which is mentioned over a dozen times in the Bible.

4 And therefore God judged them with great judgment, and they weep for their brethren and they will be punished on the Lord's great day.
5 And I said to the Grigori: I saw your brethren and their works, and their great torments, and I prayed for them, but the Lord has

condemned them to be under earth until this heaven and this earth shall end for ever.

6 And I said: Why do you stand there, brethren, and do not serve before the Lord's face, and have not put your services before the Lord's face? You could anger your Lord completely.

7 And they listened to my advice, and spoke to the four ranks in heaven. As I stood with those two men four trumpets sounded together with a loud voice, and the Grigori broke into song with one voice, and their voice went up before the Lord pitifully and touchingly.

After the insurrection of the angels was put down, El took those who remained and gave them sections of the earth to govern. The Bible tells of the god El, the supreme god or commander, who divided the areas of the earth into seventy sections, corresponding to the 70 known nations of the time, and portioned them out to his seventy "children". Israel, its land and people, were assigned to the deity Yahweh who was called Adonai, or Master. Yahweh is a personal name. Adonai is a title. Israel was his to tend as he wished. The following is taken from the Complete Jewish Bible:

Deuteronomy 32: 8 "When 'Elyon (El, god, all mighty) gave each nation its heritage, when he divided the human race, he assigned the boundaries of peoples according to Isra'el's population; 9 but ADONAI's share was his own people, Ya'akov (Jacob) his allotted heritage. 10 "He found his people in desert country, in a howling, wasted wilderness. He protected him and cared for him, guarded him like the pupil of his eye, **11** like an eagle that stirs up her nest, hovers over her young, spreads out her wings, takes them and carries them as she flies. **12** "ADONAI alone led his people; no alien god was with him. **13** He made them ride on the heights of the earth. They ate the produce of the fields. He had them suck honey from the rocks and olive oil from the crags, **14** curds from the cows and milk from the sheep, with lamb fat, rams from Bashan and goats, with the finest wheat flour; and you drank sparkling wine from the blood of grapes. **15** "But Yeshurun (the upright one – a name for Israel) grew fat and kicked (you grew fat, thick, gross!). He abandoned God his Maker; he scorned the Rock, his salvation. **16** They roused him to jealousy with alien gods, provoked him with abominations. **17** They sacrificed to demons, non-gods, gods that they had never known, new gods that had come up lately, which your ancestors had not feared. **18** You ignored the Rock who fathered you, you forgot God, who gave you birth. **19** "ADONAI saw and was filled with scorn at his sons' and daughters' provocation. **20** He said, 'I will hide my face from them and see what will become of them; for they are a perverse generation, untrustworthy children. **21** They aroused my jealousy with a non-god and provoked me with their vanities; I will arouse their jealousy with a non-people and provoke them with a vile nation. **22** "For my anger has been fired up. It burns to the depths of Sh'ol (Sh'ol or Sheol is the place of the dead. Both good and bad souls were said to be kept there. Later the Greek idea of Hades would eclipse Sheol), devouring the earth and its crops, kindling the very roots of the hills. **23** I will heap disasters on them and use up all my arrows against them. **24** "'Fatigued by hunger, they will be consumed by fever and bitter defeat; I will send them the fangs of wild beasts, and the poison of reptiles crawling in the dust. **25** Outside, the sword makes parents childless; inside, there is panic, as young men and girls alike are slain, sucklings and graybeards together. **26** "'I considered putting an end to them, erasing their memory from the human race; **27** but I feared the insolence of their enemy, feared that their foes would mistakenly think, "We ourselves accomplished this; ADONAI had nothing to do with it." **28** "'They are a nation without common sense, utterly lacking in discernment. **29** If they were wise they could figure it out and understand their destiny.

Note the name of Adonai in the text. This is actually a title, meaning "Master" and is being used to differentiate El or Elyon from the god who took Israel as his portion. Since this god is now over the Jews they refer to him as Master or Adonai. The name of this Master is Yahweh. In the scripture the Master is complaining about Israel fighting against his control and rebelling against his ultimate authority. For their disobedience he promises to turn them against one another and introduce sickness to kill those whose free will has surpassed the control El wrote into the genetic code. This may be the expression of the alien DNA or a mutation he wished to suppress. In the last paragraph he is debating how to do this and make sure everyone knows he did it. He is angry enough that he wants to wipe the memory of them but he also wants everyone to know he did it and believes they are still too stupid to comprehend everything.

26 "'I considered putting an end to them, erasing their memory from the human race; 27 but I feared the insolence of their enemy, feared that their foes would mistakenly think, "We ourselves accomplished this; ADONAI had nothing to do with it." 28 "'They are a nation without common sense, utterly lacking in discernment. 29 If they were wise they could figure it out and understand their destiny.

The numerous names for God have been a source of debate among biblical scholars. Elohim (god, or authority, plural form), El (mighty one, Adonai (master), Elyon (highest), Avinu (our father). Jewish sources accept the fact that there are various names of God used in the Hebrew Bible, and that Elohim is a plural word may suggest a polytheistic origin.

The name Yahweh occurs 6828 times in the Old Testament but somewhere around 500 BC the Jews began to believe it to be an insult to their God to use what they considered to be his personal name. The Jews stopped speaking it about 400 to 350 BC and Yahweh was replaced with "Adonai" ("My Lord or Master") while being read out loud. When the Old Testament was translated into Greek (300 BC), Yahweh was translated from Adonai which is kurios/κύριος (Lord) in Greek.

So, how would our Old Testament look to us if God's name were actually translated? Let's take a look at the Shema (Deuteronomy 6:4).

Hear, O Israel: The LORD is our God, the LORD is one.

If we include the name of God in the verse as it actually appears in the Hebrew, then it would be translated:

Hear, O Israel: Yahweh is our God, Yahweh is one.

"Do not worship any other god, for the Lord (Yahweh), whose name is jealous, is a jealous god" (Exodus 34:14)

But wait – we have a problem. We know the word Elohim is the masculine plural form of the word and thus means "Gods" but it also turns out that Adonai is a masculine plural form and thus means "Masters or Lords (as in to lord over someone). So, when the God, El, gave Israel to their Adonai or Masters the control was given to Yahweh but he may have had another "god" helping him.

Other Gods are mentioned in the scriptures, such as Ashima, Baal, Bel, Chemosh, Dagon, Milcom, Nebo, Nibhaz, Rimmon, Tammuz.

These gods and their kind were known and recognized throughout the world. Various pictographs of the same types of creatures are found in caves around the earth, painted by people in cultures that were isolated from one another.

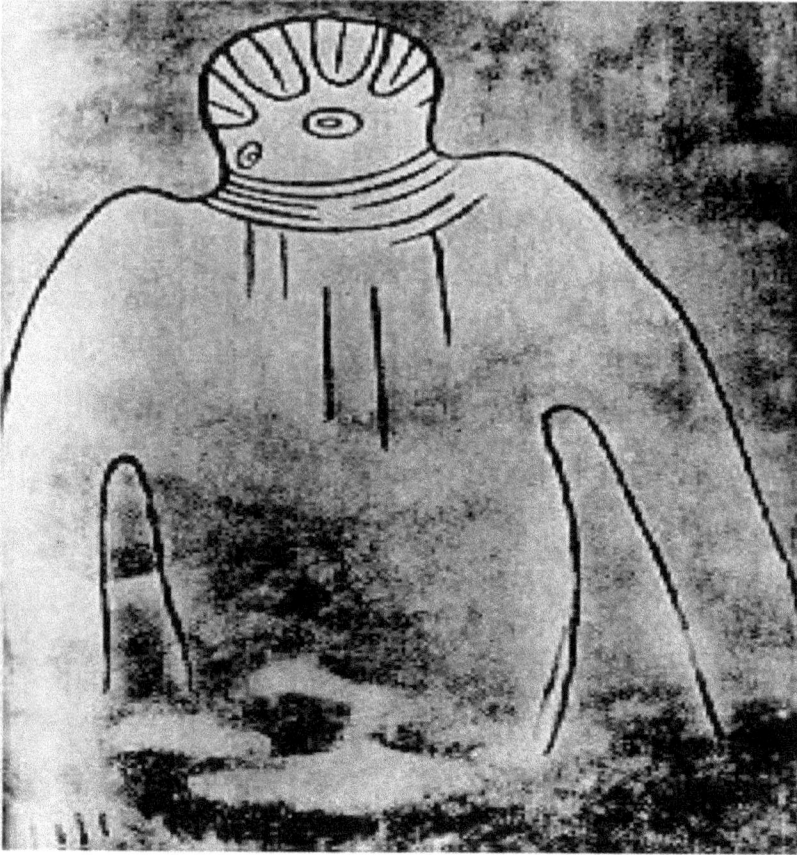

1)   6000 BC from Tassili Mountains

Let this sink in – The date of the following drawing is 6000 BC.

Putting this in perspective, around 6000 BC early people settled in

the Nile valley. Egyptians began to use clay and silt from the river

to make pottery vessels. People had just begun to farm wheat or

rice and raise livestock, such as chickens, sheep, or pigs.

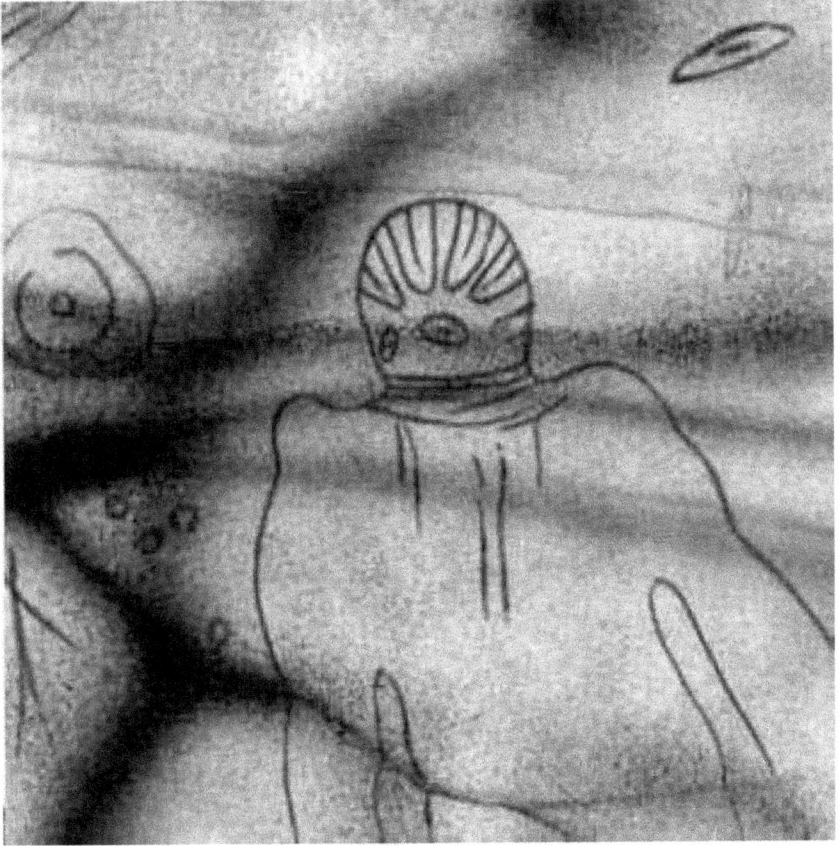

2) *Sahara Desert c. 6000 BC*

A humanoid form appearing to wear a space suit or diving suit.

3) *North Africa: A humanoid shape with the head of a sun worn like a helmet with lights. This is much the same as astronauts wear today.*

Egyptian hieroglyphs depict images carved in stone resembling the shapes of a helicopter, airplane, and spaceship.

The mo'ai, or Moai, are monolithic human figures from rock located on the Chilean Polynesian island of Easter Island between the years 1250 and 1500. Nearly half are still at Rano Raraku, the main moai quarry, but hundreds were transported from there and set on stone platforms called ahu around the island's perimeter. Almost all moai have overly large heads three-fifths the size of their bodies. The moai are chiefly the living faces (aringa ora) of deities. The debate is over how they were cared, by whom were they carved, and who or what were the deities. Were the deities ancestors of aliens?

Did ancient aliens have had a role in the creation of the moai, the statues of Easter Island? A theory holds that a spacecraft crashed on Easter Island and the aliens created the statues with as a signal to their rescuers. However, they were found and left before erecting some of the moai. This explains why some of the moai are left fallen.

Sego Canyon, Utah, c. 5,500 BC
Several figures, resembling the other humanoid forms, which
appear to be wearing a space suit or breathing apparatus.

Here, we must take stock in the stories of god, mankind, and the angelic fall. The stories make more sense if cast in the light of an alien commander, his mission, and the mutiny of his soldiers instead of an omnipotent god who did not realize his creation or his angels would turn against him.

El, the leader and commander of an alien mission landed on earth with officers and soldiers. The mission was to examine and monitor the indigenous race of humanoids, which had previously

been created or improved. The soldiers of El broke protocol.
Instead of observing the humans the soldiers began raping the
population. The commander decided to leave the soldiers in the
land they mutinied in. After a while he allowed them back into his
army but placed them in prison. Since the atrocities committed
against the population introduced genetic anomalies as well as
social stresses on the population the commander had to act to
mitigate the actions. As far-fetched as this sounds, it is not so far
from the insanity happening with earthly troupes today. We will
examine the supporting data and attempt to surmise the reason
for the alien's interest in the humanoids of earth.

Knowledge of Aliens and Gods

The scenario of alien creators is upheld by the realization that knowledge somehow given to an ancient people thousands of years prior to the present was discovered by our modern science only a few years ago. The primitive tribes could know such information by no other means than by an advanced civilization teaching them. Oral traditions of very old cultures contain such knowledge as could only be explained by being visited by advanced beings.

There are cultures whose oral traditions go back to the times of the cave drawings shown before. The teachings passed down from priest to priest tell of visitors from the stars, who taught them about stars now known but that are far too distant to be seen by the naked eye. When the Dogon left Egypt and migrated to Mali they brought with them sacred knowledge in the form of oral traditions about interaction with Amphibious Gods who came to Earth from the star Sirius (now called Sirius A). The priests also describe the shape of DNA.

The Dogon are an ethnic group located mainly in Mali, West Africa.
The precise origin of the Dogon, like those of many other ancient cultures, is undetermined. Their civilization simply emerged from

the surrounding peoples.

Their early history is recorded by oral traditions with various clans telling their versions of the story.

The people call themselves 'Dogon' or 'Dogom', but in the older literature they are most often called 'Habe', a Fulbe word meaning 'stranger' or 'pagan'.

Certain theories suggest the tribe to be of ancient Egyptian descent. They next migrated to Libya, then to Mauritania, and finally around 1490 AD they migrated to central Mali.

According to Dogon mythology, Nommo was the first living being created by Amma, the sky god and creator of the universe.

He soon multiplied to become six pairs of twins. The pattern, when drawn, turns out to be a linear pattern of the path of Sirius B around Sirius A and resembles DNA.

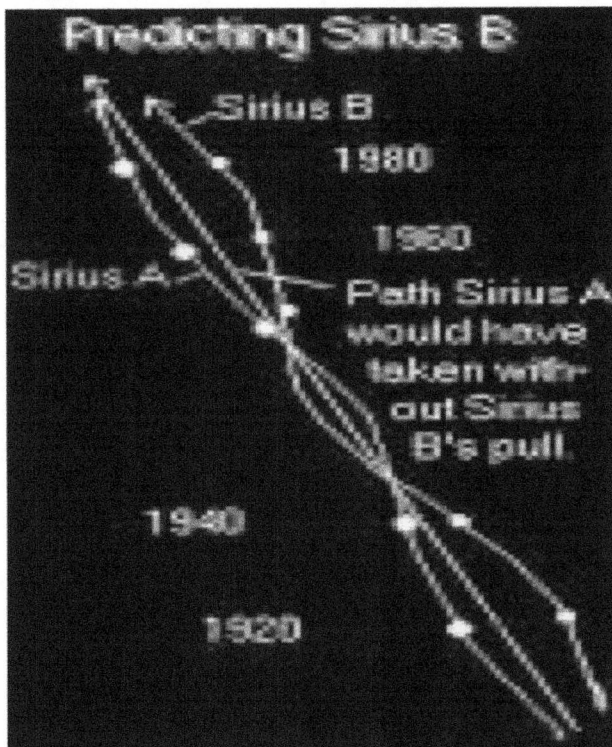

Note the centerline is a reference baseline only. The paths of the two stars form the pattern of the DNA spiral. The Dogon knew and could draw this pattern.

One twin rebelled against the order established by Amma, and thus the universe became chaotic. This story could have also been represented in the story of Cain and Abel. This part of the story reduces the structure to the two ribbons of our DNA. In order to purify the cosmos and restore its order, Amma sacrificed another of the Nommo, whose body was cut up and scattered throughout the universe. This distribution of the parts of the Nommo's body is seen as the source for the proliferation of Binu shrines throughout the Dogon region but is also a metaphor for the life scattered throughout the universe by their god.

The Dogon say that their astronomical knowledge was given to them by the Nommo.

The legend of the arrival of a divine being or Nommo has been told to a French team of scientists. The Nommo were amphibious beings sent to Earth from the Sirius star system for the benefit of humankind. This description of merman like beings match the cave drawings presented earlier.

There was a great noise as the craft came spiraling toward the earth. It skidded to a stop on three legs, burning the earth. The ship was sent from the tenth planet or moon of their star system and landed near the Dogon civilization where it was moved by something with four legs or wheels into a low lying area. The area was made into a pond or lake, which was filled with water until the vessel floated in. The Dogon, call this spaceship 'Pelu Tolo' or 'Star of the Tenth Moon'. The Dogon drew a picture of the spaceship hovering in the sky, spurting fire, waiting for the Nommo who landed on the Earth.

At the same time a new star was seen in the sky, which possibly was a large space ship. The star was described by the Dogon as having a circle of reddish rays around it. This circle of rays spread but the craft remained the same size.

This later came to be depicted as a space man with rays coming from the head area.

They called the Nommo 'Masters of the Water', 'The Monitors', 'The Teachers or Instructors', 'Saviors', and 'Spiritual Guardians'. The Dogons believed their gods were already here, having already come in alien for and still living among us.

The Dogons knew about Sirius long before modern man discovered the star system. Their religious tradition dates back to their Egyptian roots.

In the late 1930s, four Dogon priests shared their most important secret tradition with two French anthropologists, Marcel Griaule and Germain Dieterlen after they had spent an apprenticeship of fifteen years living with the tribe.

These were secret myths about the star Sirius, which is 8.6 light years from the Earth.

The priests said that Sirius had a companion star that was invisible to the human eye. The star moved in a 50-year elliptical orbit around Sirius, but it was small and incredibly heavy, and it rotated on its axis.

The anthropologists published their paper in an anthropological journal, and ignored the astronomical importance of the information, thinking it was simply a myth. What they didn't know was that since 1844, astronomers had suspected that Sirius A had a companion star. This was in part determined when it was observed that the path of the star wobbled. In 1862 Alvan Clark discovered the second star making Sirius a binary star system (two stars).

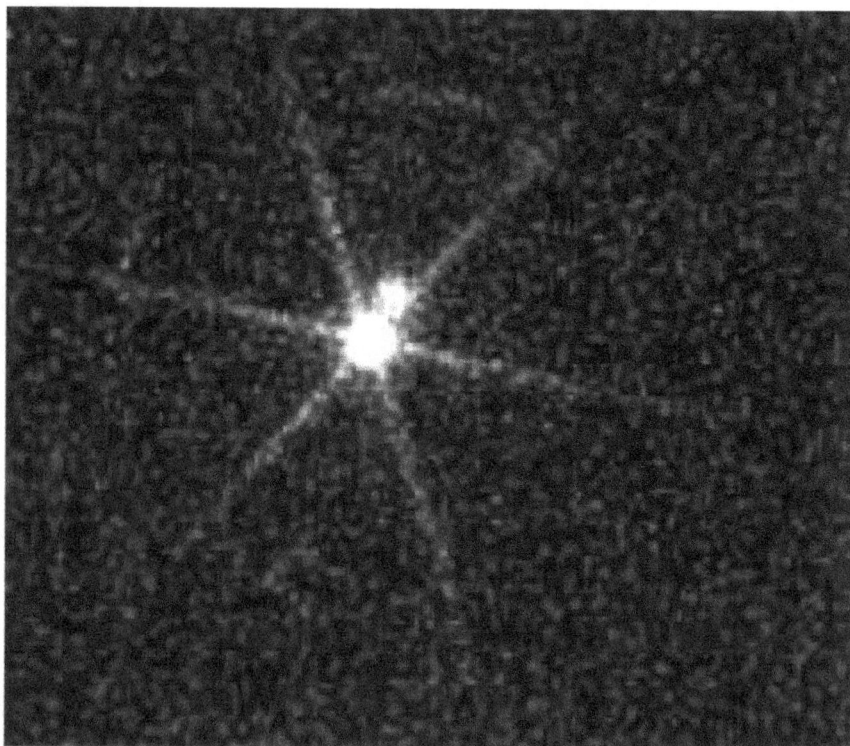

Here is a picture of Sirius A and B.

In the 1920's it was determined that Sirius B, the companion of Sirius, was a white dwarf star. White dwarfs are small, dense stars that burn dimly. The pull of its gravity causes Sirius' wavy movement. Sirius B is smaller than planet Earth.

The Dogon name for Sirius B is Po Tolo. Tolo means star and Po means a small seed. The Seed refers to creation. In this case - human creation. By this name they describe the star's smallness. It is, they say, the smallest thing there is. They also claim that it is the heaviest star and is white in color. The Dogon thus attribute to Sirius B its three principal properties as a white dwarf: small, heavy, white.

The earliest Egyptians believed Sirius - 'Sothis' - was the home of souls that have crossed over. This belief is also shared with the Dogon.

Ancient civilizations named the planets and created myths about them, all linked to the heavens and gods who created humans and came to Earth from the sky. Not far from the Pleaides, the sky is viewed like a giant map of messages. Constellations form patterns of creation.

The Dogon also claimed that a third star Emme Ya - sorghum female - exists in the Sirius system. Larger and lighter than Sirius B, this star revolves around Sirius A as well. It has not been proven to exist.

Sirius C translated from the Dogon language into English is called the "Sun of Women". It is described by the Dogon as "the seat of the female souls of living or future beings". Its symbol contains two pair of lines that are relevant features of a Dogon legend. The Dogon believe that Sirius C sends out two pairs of beams.

Dogon oral traditions state that for thousands of years they have known that the Earth revolves around the Sun, that Jupiter has moons and that Saturn has rings.

The Dogons calendar is quite non-traditional in that its fifty year cycle is based neither on the Earth's rotation around the Sun (as is our Julian calendar) nor the cycles of the Moon (a lunar calendar). Instead, the Dogon culture centers around the rotational cycle of Sirius B which encircles the primary star Sirius A every 49.9 - or 50 years. This is the exact cycle used in the Book of Jubilees to break time up into 50 year cycles call Jubilees. The Book of Jubilees is in the Ethiopic Christian Bible.

The Dogon are not the only ancient people who recorded alien visitors. In 1938 high in the mountains of BayanKara-Ula, on the borders of China and Tibet a team of archaeologists were conducting a routine survey of a series of interlocking caves.

They discovered lines of neatly arranged graves, which contained the skeletons of human-like creatures. They had frail, spindly bodies and very large heads.

At first it had been thought that the caves had been the home to an unknown species of ape. However the bodies were buried, so a civilized culture was at work here.

While studying the skeletons the team stumbled on a large round stone disc half buried in the dust on the floor of the cave.

There was a hole in the center of the stone and a spiral groove from the outside edge into the center. Within the grooves was a line of tiny, closely written characters.

For 20 years many experts in Peking tried to translate the disc. Finally Dr. Tsum Um Nui broke the code and deciphered the message.

It told the story of a "space probe" sent by the inhabitants of another planet who came to the Baya-Kara-Ula mountain range. They had crash landed. Their peaceful intentions had been misinterpreted. Many of them had been hunted down and killed by members of the Han tribe, who lived in the neighboring caves.

They referred to themselves as the Dropas. Their craft crashed, landing damaged in the mountains. They had no way to repair the ship and were thus stranded in an inhospitable place inhabited by violent creatures – man.

Dr. Tsum was ridiculed by the scientific community and later retreated from China to Japan, where he died. It is thought that Tsum was the Japanese adaptation of his real name, since that name is not Chinese.

Even though the doctor was scoffed at, there are myths that point to the truth of his discovery. Local legends spoke of small gaunt yellow faced men who came from the clouds long ago. The men had huge heads and frail bodies. They were not normal. They were so ugly they were hunted down and killed. This description is similar to the bodies found in the caves.

On the walls of the caves archaeologists found crude pictures of the rising Sun, the Moon, and stars set in constellations not appropriate to this area of space. The sun, moon, stars and the earth are all joined by lines of small dots of unknown material. The cave drawings have been dated around 12,000 years ago.

The cave area is still inhabited by 2 tribes known as the Hans and the Dropas. These tribes are odd looking in appearance. They are frail and stunted in growth, averaging only about 5 feet in height. They are neither Chinese nor Tibetan.

Aliens, Angels, and Gods

Star Maps

Below is a star map of the Pleiades, also known as the constellation of the Seven Sisters. Pleione Atlas is the tip of the arrow pointing its way to our sun.

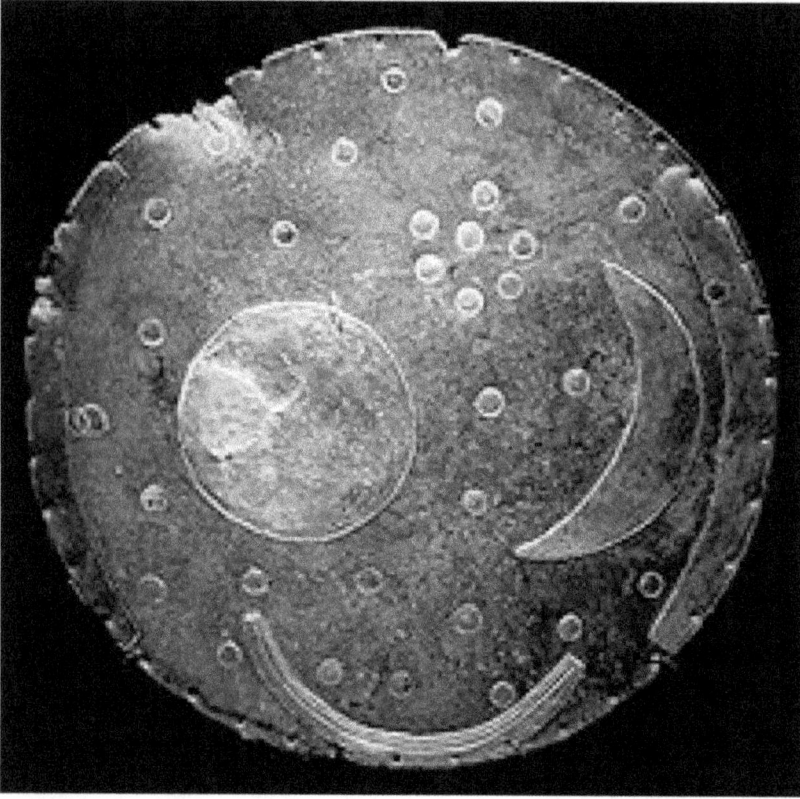

The Nebra sky disk, dated c. 1600 BC. The cluster of dots near the upper right portion of the disk is believed to be the Pleiades.

The Pleiades are a prominent sight in winter in the Northern Hemisphere and in summer in the Southern Hemisphere, and have been known since antiquity to cultures all around the world, including the Māori, Aboriginal Australians, the Persians, the Chinese, the Japanese, the Maya, the Aztec, and the Sioux and Cherokee. In Tamil culture this star cluster is attributed to Lord Murugan (Lord Murugan raised by the six sisters known as the Kārththikai Pengal and thus came to be known as Kārtikeyan), in Sanskrit he is noted as Skanda.

The Babylonian star catalogues name them MUL.MUL or "star of stars", and they head the list of stars along the ecliptic, reflecting the fact that they were close to the point of vernal equinox around the 23rd century BC. The earliest known depiction of the Pleiades is likely a bronze age artifact known as the Nebra sky disk, dated to approximately 1600 BC. Some Greek astronomers considered them to be a distinct constellation, and they are mentioned by Hesiod, and in Homer's Iliad and Odyssey.

They are also mentioned three times in the Bible (Job 9:9 and 38:31, as well as Amos 5:8). The Pleiades (Krittika) are particularly revered in Hindu mythology as the six mothers of the war god Murugan, who developed six faces, one for each of them. Some scholars of Islam suggested that the Pleiades (Ats-tsuraiya) are the Star in Najm, which is mentioned in the Quran.

In Japan, the constellation is mentioned under the name Mutsuraboshi ("six stars") in the 8th century Kojiki and Manyosyu documents. The constellation is also known in Japan as Subaru ("unite") and is depicted in the logo of the Subaru automobile company. The Persian equivalent is Nahid (pronounced "Naheed").

The rising of the Pleiades is mentioned in the Ancient Greek text Geoponica.[8] The Greeks oriented the Hecatompedon temple of

45

1150 BC and the Parthenon of 438 BC to their rising.

It looks like the first 7 Christian Churches were set in the same
pattern as the 7 Sisters.

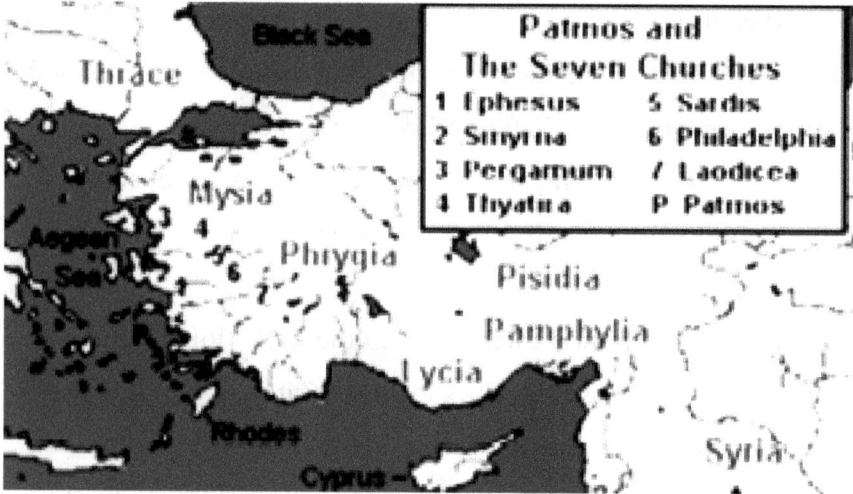

Throughout the Early World, aliens and angels were linked with
the Pleiades. These stars played an important role in many
religions. Several early calendars were regulated by them and
they were universally linked with periodical or yearly renewal.
Hammurapi ,who ruled Babylon somewhere between 1900 and
1704 B.C. was one well known Babylonian rulers. He designed a
calendar, of which the month corresponded to the 'Seven Stars', or
Pleiades. After the end of the Pleiades month, the New Year began
and during the rituals of renewal, the priests read the Creation
text which explained that after the creation of man, the Annunaki
built Babylon's great temple the Esagali.

The Annunaki were claimed to have taught primitive people about agriculture. Their apparent link with the Pleiades may be the reason why these stars were universally associated with the agricultural cycle and why they were shown on early Middle Eastern plaques with agricultural activity. One Assyrian plaque shows the Pleiades above seven figures who appear to have been based on the Annunaki leaders.

The Pleiades were linked with the Creation in many early cultures. Many civilizations believed departed souls were returned to Earth, among them were the Celts, and civilizations in Mexico and Peru. The Celts called it Samain and it began with the rising of the Pleiades when the gates of the Otherworld were open and when new fires were lit. This festival was later adopted by the Church and observed around the world as All Hallows. Its also now popularly celebrated as Halloween.

The Mayas believed that 'sky-people'came here around 5,000 years ago. Their arrival resulted in a catastrophic upheaval which completely disrupted life all over the planet. After they had finished their destruction they re-seeded civilizations, which arose as cities and states, fully developed. Sumerians arrived in their country in Southern Iraq and claimed to be survivors of the Flood. This era was the beginning of the present age.

In the Bible story, Job was extremely wealthy and had a happy, healthy family. But, tragedy struck and he lost his wealth, his children and his wife. They died. To make matters worse, Job was reduced to excruciating pain, and was eventually covered with sores from head to toe. All of this was brought about by an angel called the "deceiver." Job eventually accused the Lord of being unjust. God reminded Job He was in control by asking Job a series of questions. These questions demonstrates scientific truth in scripture:

Job 38:31-32
Canst thou bind the sweet influences of Pleiades, or loose the bands of Orion? Canst thou bring forth Mazzaroth in his season? or canst thou guide Arcturus with his sons?

God makes a statement about three stellar constellations by asking directed questions:
'Canst thou . . . loose the bands of Orion?' God is talking specifically about the three stars that form the belt on the Orion constellation. He is telling Job these stars can be rearranged only by God. These three stars appeared to be fixed on our sky, rigidly aligned to form a relatively straight line but God asked Job if he can alter this arrangement. Today, this band consists of an almost perfectly straight line of second-magnitude stars that are equally spaced and very beautiful.

In the course of time, however, the two right-hand stars, Mintaka and Alnilam, will approach each other and form a naked-eye double; but the third, Alnitak, will drift away eastward so that the band will no longer exist. In other words, one star is traveling in a certain direction at a certain speed, a second one is traveling in a different direction at a second speed, and the third one is going in a third direction and at a still different speed. As a matter of fact, every star in Orion is traveling its own course, independent of all the others. As time passes, this band of stars will indeed be loosened, just as God told Job.

Then God says: 'Canst thou bind the sweet influence of the Pleiades . . . ?' God is challenging Job saying, "Do you think you can keep Pleiades together?" The seven stars of the Pleiades are in reality a grouping of 250 suns. And photographs now reveal, that 250 blazing suns in this group are all traveling together in one common direction. Isabel Lewis of the United States Naval Observatory (quoted in Phillip L. Knox', "Wonder Worlds") tells us that astronomers have identified 250 stars as actual members of this group, all sharing a common motion and drifting through space in the same direction. Lewis says they are 'journeying onward together through the immensity of space.' Multiple measurements, taken over time, shows the whole cluster is moving in a southeasterly direction. The Pleiades stars are kind of like a swarm of birds, flying together to a distant goal.

Finally, God asks, 'Canst thou guide Arcturus with his sons?' Arcturus may look like it is fixed in the sky, but Garrett P. Serviss wrote that Arcturus is one of the greatest suns in the universe, and it is a runaway star whose speed of flight is about 257 miles per second. Arcturus, according to astronomers, is thousands of times more massive than our sun, which is traveling only 12 ½ miles a second! Charles Burckhalter, of the Chabot Observatory, (again quoted in "Wonder Worlds") says that Arcturus' high velocity places it in that very small class of stars that apparently are a law unto themselves.

The question, of course, is how the writers of the book of Job, which is the oldest book in the Bible, would know these things.

The Bible goes on to say:
Amos 5:8
Seek him that makes the seven stars (Pleiades) and Orion, and turns the shadow of death into the morning, and makes the day dark with night: that calls for the waters of the sea, and pours them out upon the face of the earth: The LORD is his name:

Job 9:9
Which maketh Arcturus, Orion, and Pleiades, and the chambers of the south.

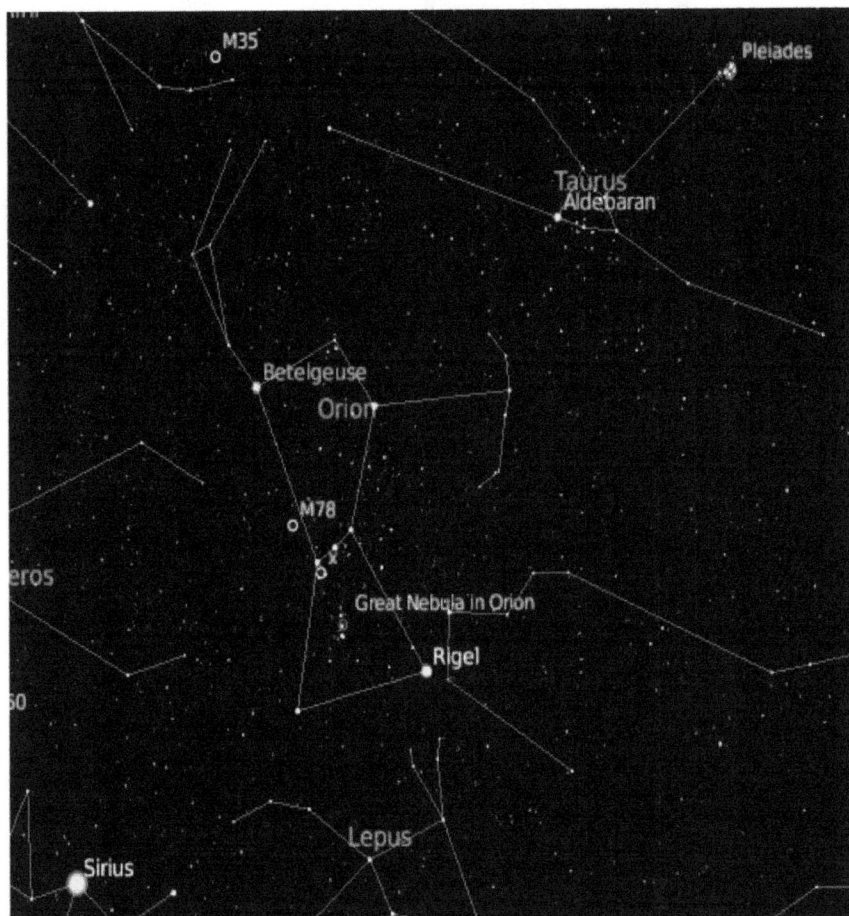

The sky map above shows the relationship of Sirius to the Pleiades. Note Orion lays directly between them.

Some myths and traditions claim visitors came from an area of space around Sirius. Some claim they arrived from the area of space around the Pleiades. All agree these beings arrived in flying machines – spaceships. These crafts were drawn on cave walls, and spoken of in religious texts.

Ancient flying machines have long been a tradition of many cultures across the globe, including Hindu texts such as the Ramayana.

"Vidyutkesha, that ranger of the night, having received the daughter of Sandhya, began to divert himself with her. After a time, O Rama, Salatantaka was filled with child, as a cloud is charged with water from the ocean.

Repairing to the Mandara Mountain, the Rakshasi (Salatantaka) brought forth a child who was as beautiful as a cloud, even as Ganga had been delivered of an infant by the god of fire. Having given birth to that child, who was named Sukesha, she again desired to disport herself with Vidyutkesha and, forsaking her son, she rejoined her consort. Then the infant who had just been born and was as radiant as the autumnal sun, whose voice resembled the rumbling of a cloud, placing his fist in his mouth cried for a long time, and Shiva, who was following the path of the Wind, mounted on His bull and accompanied by Parvati, heard the sound of weeping and with Parvati beheld the son of the Rakshasi who was crying. Allowing himself to be moved by compassion by His consort, Bhava (Shiva), the destroyer of Tripura, made him equal to his mother in age and bestowed immortality upon him. Thereafter the unchanging and imperishable Mahadeva (Shiva) bestowed an aerial car upon him that traversed space, in order to gratify Parvati, and she, on her side, also conferred a boon on him, saying:

'The Rakshasas shall conceive instantly and give birth as they conceive. Their children shall at once attain the age of their mothers.'

Thereafter the highly intelligent Sukesha, proud of the favours he had received, having obtained this great fortune from the Lord Hara (Shiva), began to range everywhere, displaying himself in his aerial car and resembling Purandara when he obtained heaven."

For the past two thousand years the Ramayana has been among the more important literary and oral texts of South Asia. This epic poem provides insights into many aspects of Indian culture and continues to influence the politics, religion and art of modern India.

The Mahabharata describe airships called Vamanas that were even used for battle.

The Mahabharata (composed between 300 BC and 300 AD) has the honor of being the longest epic in world literature, 100,000 2-line stanzas (although the most recent critical edition edits this down to about 88,000), making it eight times as long as Homer's Iliad and Odyssey together, and over 3 times as long as the Bible (Chaitanya vii). According to the Narasimhan version, only about 4000 lines relate to the main story; the rest contain additional myths and teachings. In other words, the Mahabharata resembles a long journey with many side roads and detours. It is said that "Whatever is here is found elsewhere. But whatever is not here is nowhere else."

The name means "great [story of the] Bharatas." Bharata was an early ancestor of both the Pandavas and Kauravas who fight each other in a great war, but the word is also used generically for the Indian race, so the Mahabharata sometimes is referred to as "the great story of India."

According to Dr.V. Raghavan, retired head of the Sanskrit department of India's prestigious University of Madras, India was host to extraterrestrials in prehistory. Dr. Raghavan contends that centuries-old documents in Sanskrit (the classical language of India and Hinduism) prove that aliens from outer space visited his nation.

"Fifty years of researching this ancient works convinces me that there are living beings on other planets, and that they visited earth as far back as 4,000 B.C.", the scholar says.

"There is a just a mass of fascinating information about flying machines, even fantastic science fiction weapons, that can be found in translations of the Vedas (scriptures), Indian epics, and other ancient Sanskrit text".

In the Mahabharata (writings), there is notion of divine lighting and ray weapons, even a kind of hypnotic weapon.

"Gurkha flying in his swift and powerful Vimana hurled against the three cities of the Vrishis and Andhakas a single projectile charged with all the power of the Universe. An incandescent column of smoke and fire, as brilliant as ten thousands suns, rose in all its splendour. It was the unknown weapon, the Iron Thunderbolt, a gigantic messenger of death which reduced to ashes the entire race of the Vrishnis and Andhakas."

India was not the only area visited by space travelers. Among the hieroglyphs on the wall of a 3,000 year-old Egyptian temple at Abydos are depictions of what appear to be modern airplanes and helicopters.

Grooved stone discs found in caves on the Chinese-Tibetan border tell of an extraterrestrial race called the Dropas whose spacecraft fell to Earth 12,000 years ago, and Hopi Indians of North America have a rich tradition of oral history telling of visits by space travelers.

In the Third Book of Enoch, also called the Hebrew Book of Enoch, we find the ascension of Enoch was conducted in a vessel, which is also referred to in the book of Ezekiel.

CHAPTER I

INTRODUCTION: Rabbi Ishmael ascends to heaven to witness the vision of the Merkaba (chariot). He is given to Metatron

AND ENOCH WALKED WITH GOD: AND HE WAS NOT; FOR GOD TOOK HIM.

(1) I ascended on high to witness the vision of the Merkaba (the divine chariot) and I had entered the six Halls, which were situated within one another.

The halls were in concentric circles, one within the other.

(2) As soon as I reached the door of the Seventh Hall I stood still in prayer before the Holy One, blessed be He. I lifted up my eyes on high towards the Divine Majesty and I said: (3) " Lord of the Universe, I pray you, that the worthiness of Aaron, the son of Amram, who loves and pursues peace, and who received the crown of priesthood from Your Glory on Mount Sinai, be upon me in this hour, so that Khafsiel, (Qafsiel) the prince, and the angels with him may not

overcome (overpower) me nor cast me down from the heavens."

Qafsiel or Qaphsiel is an angel of a high order set to guard the seventh hall of heaven

(4) At that moment the Holy One, blessed be He, sent Metatron, his Servant, also called Ebed, to me. He is the angel, the Prince of the Presence. With great joy he spread his wings as he came to meet me in order to save me from their hand. (5) And by his hand he took me so that they could see us, and he said to me: "Enter in peace before the high and exalted King and see the picture of Merkaba (chariot)."

Merkaba (chariot) – Chariot of fire, Chariot of light - Pulled by four Chayot or living creatures, each of which has four wings and the four faces of a man, lion, ox, and eagle.. See Ezekiel 1:4-26. The Bible makes mention of three types of angel found in the Merkaba (chariot) . The first is the "Seraphim" (lit. "burning") angels. These angels appear like flashes of fire continuously ascending and descending. These "Seraphim" angels powered the movement of the chariot. In the hierarchy of these angels, "Seraphim" are the highest, that is, closest to God, followed by the "Chayot", which are followed by the "Ophanim." The chariot is in a constant state of motion, and the energy behind this movement runs according to this hierarchy. The movement of the "Ophanim" are controlled by the "Chayot" while the movement of the "Chayot" is controlled by the "Seraphim." The movement of all the angels of the chariot are controlled by the "Likeness of a Man" on the Throne.

(6) Then I entered the seventh Hall, and he led me to the camps of Shekina (understanding) and stood me in front of the Holy One, blessed be He, to see the Merkaba (chariot).

Ophanim are described in 1 Enoch as never sleeping. They watch and guard the throne of God. The word ophan means "wheel" in Hebrew. For this reason the Ophanim have been associated with the chariot in Ezekiel and Daniel. It is mentioned as gagal, traditionally "the wheels of gagallin", in "fiery flame" and "burning fire" of the four, eye-covered wheels, each composed of two nested wheels, that move next to the winged Cherubim, beneath the throne of God. The four wheels move with the Cherubim because the spirit of the Cherubim is in them. These are also referred to as the "many-eyed ones" in 2 Enoch. The Ophanim are also equated as the "Thrones", and associated with the "Wheels", in the vision of Daniel 7:9. They carry the throne of God, hence the name.

(9) Then Metatron, the Prince of the Presence, came and placed my spirit in me again and he stood me up on my feet. (10) After that (moment) for an hour I did not have enough strength to sing a song before the Throne of Glory of the

Glorious King, the mightiest of all kings, the most excellent of all princes. (11) After an hour had passed the Holy One, blessed be He, opened the gates of Shekina (understanding) to me. These are the gates of Peace, and of Wisdom, and of Strength, and of Power, and of Speech (Dibbur), and of Song, and of Kedushah (Sacred Salutation of Holy, Holy, Holy), and the gates of Chanting. (12) And he opened and shined His light in my eyes and my heart by words of psalm, song, praise, exaltation, thanksgiving, extolment, glorification, hymn and eulogy (to speak well of). And as I opened my mouth, singing a song before the Holy One, blessed be He the Holy Chayoth beneath and above the Throne of Glory answered and said (chanted the prayer): "HOLY!" "BLESSED BE THE GLORY OF YHWH FROM HIS PLACE!."

The Chayot (or Chayyot) are a class of Merkabah, or Jewish Mystical Angels, reported in Ezekeil's vision of the Merkabah and its surrounding angels as recorded in the first chapter of the Book of Ezekiel describing his vision by the river Chebar.

Here is the description found in the Book of Ezekiel.
Ezekiel 1
New King James Version (NKJV)
Ezekiel's Vision of God

1 Now it came to pass in the thirtieth year, in the fourth month, on the fifth day of the month, as I was among the captives by the River Chebar, that the heavens were opened and I saw visions[a] of God. 2 On the fifth day of the month, which was in the fifth year of King Jehoiachin's captivity, 3 the word of the Lord came expressly to Ezekiel the priest, the son of Buzi, in the land of the Chaldeans[b] by the River Chebar; and the hand of the Lord was upon him there.

4 Then I looked, and behold, a whirlwind was coming out of the north, a great cloud with raging fire engulfing itself; and brightness was all around it and radiating out of its midst like the color of amber, out of the midst of the fire. 5 Also from within it came the likeness of four living creatures. And this was their appearance: they had the likeness of a man. 6 Each one had four faces, and each one had four wings. 7 Their legs were straight, and the soles of their feet were like the soles of calves' feet. They sparkled like the color of burnished bronze. 8 The hands of a man were under their wings on their four sides; and each of the four had faces and wings. 9 Their wings touched one another. The creatures did not turn when they went, but each one went straight forward.

10 As for the likeness of their faces, each had the face of a man; each of the four had the face of a lion on the right side, each of the four had the face of an ox on the left side, and each of the four had the face of an eagle. 11 Thus were their faces. Their wings stretched upward; two wings of each one touched one another, and two covered their bodies. 12 And each one went straight forward; they went wherever the spirit wanted to go, and they did not turn when they went.

13 As for the likeness of the living creatures, their appearance was like burning coals of fire, like the appearance of torches going back and forth among the living creatures. The fire was bright, and out of the fire went lightning. 14 And the living creatures ran back and forth, in appearance like a flash of lightning.

15 Now as I looked at the living creatures, behold, a wheel was on the earth beside each living creature with its four faces. 16 The appearance of the wheels and their workings was like the color of beryl, and all four had the same likeness. The appearance of their workings was, as it were, a wheel in the middle of a wheel. 17 When they moved, they went toward any one of four directions; they did not turn aside when they went. 18 As for their rims, they were so high they were awesome; and their rims were full of eyes, all around the four of them. 19 When the living creatures went, the wheels went beside them; and when the living creatures were lifted up from the earth, the wheels were lifted up. 20 Wherever the spirit wanted to go, they went, because there the spirit went; and the wheels were lifted together with them, for the spirit of the living creatures[c] was in the wheels. 21 When those went, these went; when those stood, these stood; and when those were lifted up from the earth, the wheels were lifted up together with them, for the spirit of the living creatures[d] was in the wheels.

22 The likeness of the firmament above the heads of the living creatures[e] was like the color of an awesome crystal, stretched out over their heads. 23 And under the firmament their wings spread out straight, one toward another. Each one had two which covered one side, and each one had two which covered the other side of the body. 24 When they went, I heard the noise of their wings, like the noise of many waters, like the voice of the Almighty, a tumult like the noise of an army; and when they stood still, they let down their wings. 25 A voice came from above the firmament that was over their heads; whenever they stood, they let down their wings.

26 And above the firmament over their heads was the likeness of a throne, in appearance like a sapphire stone; on the likeness of the throne was a likeness with the appearance of a man high above it. 27 Also from the appearance of His waist and upward I saw, as it were, the color of amber with the appearance of fire all around within it; and from the appearance of His waist and downward I saw, as it were, the appearance of fire with brightness all around. 28 Like the appearance of a rainbow in a cloud on a rainy day, so was the appearance of the brightness all around it. This was the appearance of the likeness of the glory of the Lord.

Holy books are not the only accounts of flying craft. The Native Americans have their legends of alien visits as well.

The Hopi Indians have inhabited three large mesas in northern Arizona for over a thousand years. Their legends also refer to aerial vehicles, perhaps from Orion.

The Hopi may have settled on the three primary mesas in Arizona because they wanted to reflect their star elders' constellation of origin. (See The OrionZone by Gary A. David.)

These magical flying shields called "paatuwvota" existed in the Third World, a previous period of time which came to an end when the world was destroyed by a great flood. This was a time when great cities and trade routes were built, and civilization was flourishing.

In an address delivered to the United Nations, Thomas Banyacya of the Hopi Coyote Clan said: "The people invented many machines and conveniences of high technology, some of which have not yet been seen in this age."

In one legend the flying shield is associated with Sotuknang, the Hopi sky god. A flood had destroyed Palatkwapi, "the red city to the south" possibly located near Sedona, Arizona. In the ensuing chaos a brother named Tiwahongva and his sister Tawiayisnima, were forgotten and left behind by their fleeing parents. They would have to journey blindly to find them.

In the evening they decided to make camp. As they opened the bundle of their meager supplies they heard a loud roar coming from above. The children were frightened and the brother held his sister tightly to protect her. A being emerged from a craft, which had descended and landed. He was wearing a uniform that glittered like ice and his head and face shone like a star. He spoke: "Do not be afraid. My name is Sotuknang. Because of my sympathy for your plight, I have come to help you. Get on my paatuwvota and we will be on our way."

He then took them on his flying shield up into the sky so that they could see for many miles around. Feeding the hungry children ripe melons, he told them that they must have faith in him and in his teachings that would later arrive through their dreams. Finally he landed a short distance from the village in which their mother and father had settled, bid the young ones farewell, and flew up again into the clouds. Forever grateful to the sky god, the brother and sister walked into the village to be reunited with their parents."

In his book Mexico Mystique, Frank Waters, a non-Indian expert on the Hopis, writes:

"On Second Mesa near Mishongnovi an ancient petroglyph depicts a dome-shaped object resting on an arrow which represent travel through space, and the head of a Hopi maiden who represents pristine purity. As the Hopis believe that other planets are inhabited, this petroglyph represents a paatuwvota or a 'flying shield' similar to a 'flying saucer' that came here in the beginning. So now at the end of days the sacred ones will arrive from another planet by way of these same flying shields. Many Hopi traditionalists recently have reported seeing flying saucers, all piloted by beings they call kachinas."

The kachinas have come to be thought of as the protectors of the Hopi. Wooden kachina dolls carved by the Hopis are used during the spring and early summer ceremonial cycles. Men wearing masks of kachina dance as a plea for rain and the general well being of the tribe.

Eototo, chief kachina (left) and Aholi, his lieutenant.
Hopi kachina dolls at Museum of Northern Arizona.

In the photograph above we see a kachina, looking very much like the cave drawings of 6000 BC. These are the same beings visiting us throughout the millennia.

Much like the fallen angels (or the Watchers) of the Bible (see Genesis 6:1-4), the kachinas were sometimes known to mate with Hopi women.

Indeed, beginning with the first cave drawings around 6000 BC and continuing today within the Hopi community and other communities, images and stories of aliens, angels or gods continue. It is very likely, and one might say a surety, that the visitations began before 6000 BC but the ability of the humanoids of that day to communicate was not yet developed, and thus the events were never recorded.

For a minimum of eight thousand years, creatures we have identified as Angels, Demons, Aliens, and Gods have been among us, visiting, manipulating, and some times mating with us.

One Hopi myth tells of a young bride who accompanies her husband back to her Second Mesa village of Mishongnovi on a flying shield.

One legend of such an intermarriage can be read in a book called "Earth Fire: A Hopi Legend of the Sunset Crater Eruption," co-authored by Ekkehart Malotki. "As the shield lifted off, the kachinas all gave out a boisterous yell. The spectacle was incredible; every sort of kachina conceivable was present. All of a sudden as the couple flew along, flashes of lightning were visible in the air and the rumble of thunder could be heard. When the shield rose higher, drizzle began to fall. The kachinas were now accompanying them... [Her] parents had headed to the edge of the mesa at this time to look out. Looking down from the rim of the mesa, they saw an incredible number of people coming across the plain. To their great amazement all were kachinas, singing and crying out their calls in a pandemonium."

To this day unexplained sightings continue in the area of the Hopi villages and throughout Arizona. In the summer of 1970 hundreds of UFOs were seen about 125 miles southwest of the Hopi villages near the town of Prescott, Arizona, known as the Phoenix Lights.

Let us remember that in the First book of Enoch there is a short list of the knowledge the visitors taught men.

[Chapter 8]
1 And Azazel taught men to make swords, and knives, and shields, and breastplates, and taught them about metals of the earth and the art of working them, and bracelets, and ornaments, and the use of antimony, and the beautifying of the eyelids, and all kinds of precious stones, and all coloring and dyes.

2 And there was great impiety, they turned away from God, and committed fornication, and they were led astray, and became corrupt in all their ways.

3 Semjaza taught the casting of spells, and root-cuttings, Armaros taught counter-spells (release from spells), Baraqijal taught astrology, Kokabel taught the constellations, Ezeqeel the knowledge of the clouds, Araqiel the signs of the earth, Shamsiel the signs of the sun, and Sariel the course of the moon.

Constellations, the signs of the sun, and the course of the moon are astrological events mentioned three times. Structures using such events are found all over the earth.

Stonehenge and other structures come to mind. Stonehenge is a prehistoric monument in the English county of Wiltshire, about 2 miles west of Amesbury and 8 miles north of Salisbury. Stonehenge is the remains of a ring of standing stones set within ditches and banks. It is in the middle of a complex of Neolithic and Bronze Age monuments in England, including several hundred burial mounds.

Archaeologists have found five large postholes, which date to around 8000 BC. This roughly coincides with the period of time we believe men began to record alien visitations.

Four posts were in an east-west alignment. Similar sites have been found in Scandinavia.

Later stone would replace the wooden posts in the building material. The first monument consisted of a circular bank and ditch enclosure made of Seaford Chalk, measuring about 360 ft in diameter, with a large entrance to the north east and a smaller one to the south. The first stage of this construction is dated to around 3100 BC, after which the ditch began to silt up naturally.

Evidence of the second phase is no longer visible. The number of postholes dating to the early 3rd millennium BC suggest that some form of timber structure was built within the enclosure during this period. Further standing timbers were placed at the northeast entrance, and a parallel alignment of posts ran inwards from the southern entrance. In this period of time they brought their dead here ot be cremated. Thirty further cremations were placed in the enclosure's ditch and at other points within the monument, mostly in the eastern half. Stonehenge was functioning as an enclosed cremation cemetery at this time, the earliest known cremation cemetery in the British Isles. Fragments of human bone have been found in the ditch. Dating evidence is provided by the late Neolithic grooved ware pottery that has been found in connection with the features from this phase.

Around 2600 BC, the builders abandoned timber in favor of stone and dug two concentric arrays. The bluestones was transported from the Preseli Hills, 150 miles away in modern-day Pembrokeshire in Wales.

There is little or no direct evidence for the construction techniques used by the Stonehenge builders.

Proposed functions for the site include usage as an astronomical observatory, or as a religious site. More recently two major new theories have been proposed. Professor Geoffrey Wainwright OBE, FSA, president of the Society of Antiquaries of London, and Professor Timothy Darvill, OBE of Bournemouth University have suggested that Stonehenge was a place of healing – the primeval equivalent of Lourdes. They argue that this accounts for the high number of burials in the area and for the evidence of trauma deformity in some of the graves. Whatever religious, mystical or spiritual elements were central to Stonehenge, its design includes a celestial observatory function, which might have allowed prediction of eclipse, solstice, equinox and other celestial events important to a contemporary religion.

Research turned up no less than 24 alignments, that is, orientations where pairs of stones seem to line up or point to the settings and risings of the sun and moon in the sky.

In the 1930s, Alexander Thom had been hiking all over the British Isles and sailing up the lochs of Scotland to survey the 900 or so other stone circles besides Stonehenge. After reviewing his data he came up with extraordinary claims that a true science of astronomy had been practiced in Britain some 4000 years ago. That their sky watching had been practiced at a truly mind-boggling level of precision, comparable to that of a modern astronomer.

It looked like a sober academic study, and suddenly, the archeological community totally changed its attitude. They took Thom's work very seriously.

Thom was measuring the sites on his surveys to within fractions of an inch. And he claimed that the ancient builders of these stones were doing the same thing. Now it is fairly well accepted that a less precise level of watching the sun and the moon almost certainly was done. That it was part of a ritual calendar system, that it was there to mark midsummer and mid winter, these key seasons in the agricultural calendar and the ritual calendar.

Emanuel Rapha

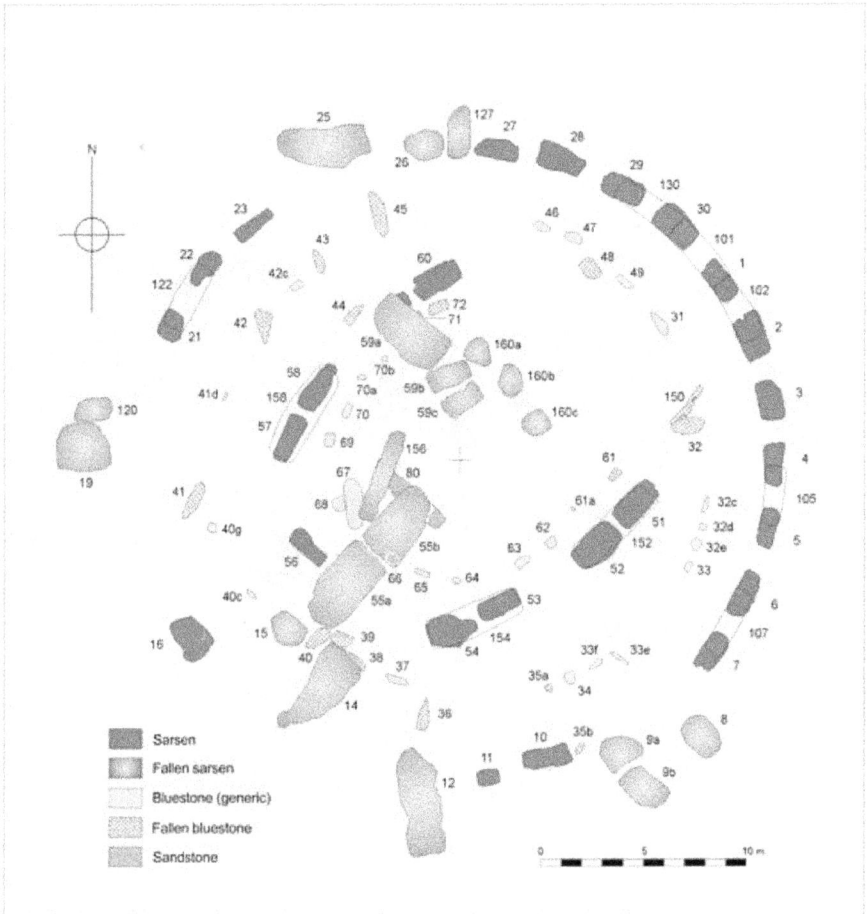

At Machu Picchu in Peru, an Inca ceremony took place during the winter solstice (June 21st in the Southern Hemisphere) to "tie the Sun" and keep it from moving too far north on its daily arc. Machu Picchu lies in the southern hemisphere, some 13 degrees south of the equator. It is 80 kilometers northwest of Cusco, on the crest of the mountain Machu Picchu, located about 2,450 metres (8,040 ft) above mean sea level, over 1,000 metres (3,300 ft) lower than Cusco, which has an altitude of 3,600 metres (11,800 ft).

Descending the hill next to this site is the Great Central Temple, a three walled building with fine stonework and an attached smaller temple called the "Sacristy". Next to this structure is another three walled building, known as the 'Temple of the Three Windows', so called because of the trapezoidal openings on the east wall. Directly across is the Royal sector, with ample buildings typical of Inca royalty. A very important structure in this section is the "Temple of the Sun", a: circular tower with the best stonework of Machu Picchu. Its base forms a cavern known as the Royal Tomb. Recent studies show that the actual purpose was for astronomical observance.

At the Great Pyramids of Egypt (built 2600 BC), an astronomer discovered that a King's burial chamber aligns with both the belt of Orion and Thuban, called the "Imperishable Star" by the ancient Egyptians. These constellations gave the pharaoh two pathways of renewal and resurrection. The study of these types of planetary alignments is called archaeoastronomy. Creation is linked to the Great Pyramid which links to Orion in the Kings Chamber (male) and to Sirius in the Queens Chamber (female), Isis. There are advanced mathematics built into the Great Pyramid. Two times the base divided by the height equals Pi (3.14159265359). The ancient Babylonians calculated the area of a circle by taking 3 times the square of its radius, which gave a value of pi = 3. One Babylonian tablet (ca. 1900–1680 BC) indicates a value of 3.125 for pi, which is a closer approximation.

Rhind Papyrus (ca.1650 BC), there is evidence that the Egyptians calculated the area of a circle by a formula that gave the approximate value of 3.1605 for pi.

The ancient cultures mentioned above found their approximations by measurement. The first calculation of pi was done by Archimedes of Syracuse (287–212 BC), one of the greatest mathematicians of the ancient world.

Archimedes approximated the area of a circle by using the

Pythagorean Theorem to find the areas of two regular polygons: the polygon inscribed within the circle and the polygon within which the circle was circumscribed. Since the actual area of the circle lies between the areas of the inscribed and circumscribed polygons, the areas of the polygons gave upper and lower bounds for the area of the circle. Archimedes knew that he had not found the value of pi but only an approximation within those limits. In this way, Archimedes showed that pi is between 3 1/7 and 3 10/71.

Building techniques, math and astronomy bloomed around the same time.

Clay tablets with astrological symbols unearthed at the site of ancient Babylon date to about 3000 B.C. The Chaldeans are thought to have spread a highly developed astrological system throughout the Middle East and Egypt.

Creation, Evolution, Betrayal

All over the world, in cultures that were isolated, the same ideas arose and the same mechanisms of detection developed to track sun, moon, and planets. Did this knowledge come to us from a more advanced race? Are these ancient aliens or astronauts the god or gods of old? Did they give man knowledge he could have had no other way? Did they come before? Did they govern us in times passed? Did they educate and teach us? Do we owe our existence to them? More to the point, did they create us or manipulate DNA of existing humanoids to produce us? Over millions of years there was little change in the population of humans, but beginning around the point of the first documented interactions between mankind and aliens visitors our acceleration began. Did it begin because of their teachings or because of their manipulation of our DNA?

1.7 million B.C.

Homo erectus leaves Africa.

100,000 B.C.

First modern *Homo sapiens* in South Africa.

70,000 B.C.

Neanderthal man (use of fire and advanced tools).

35,000 B.C.

Neanderthal man replaced by later groups of *Homo sapiens* (i.e., Cro-Magnon man, etc.).

18,000 B.C.

Cro-Magnons replaced by later cultures.

15,000 B.C.

Migrations across Bering Straits into the Americas.

10,000 B.C.

Semi-permanent agricultural settlements in Old World.

10,000–4,000 B.C.

First Alien Encounter

Development of settlements into cities and development of skills such as the wheel, pottery, and improved methods of cultivation in Mesopotamia and elsewhere.

5500–3000 B.C.

Predynastic Egyptian cultures develop (5500–3100 B.C.); begin using agriculture (c. 5000 B.C.). Earliest known civilization arises in Sumer (4500–4000 B.C.). Earliest recorded date in Egyptian calendar (4241 B.C.). First year of Jewish calendar (3760 B.C.). First phonetic writing appears (c. 3500 B.C.). Sumerians develop a city-state civilization (c. 3000 B.C.). Copper used by Egyptians and Sumerians. Western Europe is neolithic, without metals or written records.

3000–2000 B.C.

Pharaonic rule begins in Egypt. King Khufu (Cheops), 4th dynasty (2700–2675 B.C.), completes construction of the Great Pyramid at Giza (c. 2680 B.C.). The Great Sphinx of Giza (c. 2540 B.C.) is built by King Khafre. Earliest Egyptian mummies. Papyrus. Phoenician settlements on coast of what is now Syria and Lebanon. Semitic tribes settle in Assyria. Sargon, first

Akkadian king, builds Mesopotamian empire. The Gilgamesh epic (c. 3000 B.C.). Systematic astronomy in Egypt, Babylon, India, China.

3000–1500 B.C.

The most ancient civilization on the Indian subcontinent, the sophisticated and extensive Indus Valley civilization, flourishes in what is today Pakistan. In Britain, Stonehenge erected according to some unknown astronomical rationale. Its three main phases of construction are thought to span c. 3000–1500 B.C.

2000–1500 B.C.

Hyksos invaders drive Egyptians from Lower Egypt (17th century B.C.). Amosis I frees Egypt from Hyksos (c. 1600 B.C.). Assyrians rise to power—cities of Ashur and Nineveh. Twenty-four-character alphabet in Egypt. Cuneiform inscriptions used by Hittites. Peak of Minoan culture on Isle of Crete—earliest form of written Greek. Hammurabi, king of Babylon, develops oldest existing code of laws (18th centuryB.C.).

1500–1000 B.C.

Ikhnaton develops monotheistic religion in Egypt (c. 1375 B.C.). His successor, Tutankhamen, returns to earlier gods. Greeks destroy Troy (c. 1193 B.C.). End of Greek civilization in Mycenae with invasion of Dorians. Chinese civilization develops under Shang Dynasty. Olmec civilization in Mexico—stone monuments; picture writing.

1000–900 B.C.

Solomon succeeds King David, builds Jerusalem temple. After Solomon's death, kingdom divided into Israel and Judah. Hebrew elders begin to write Old Testament books of Bible. Phoenicians colonize Spain with settlement at Cadiz.

900–800 B.C.

Phoenicians establish Carthage (c. 810 B.C.). The *Iliad* and the *Odyssey,* perhaps composed by Greek poet Homer.

800–700 B.C.

Prophets Amos, Hosea, Isaiah. First recorded Olympic games (776 B.C.). Legendary founding of Rome by Romulus (753 B.C.). Assyrian king Sargon II conquers Hittites, Chaldeans, Samaria (end of Kingdom of Israel). Earliest written music. Chariots introduced into Italy by Etruscans.

700–600 B.C.

End of Assyrian Empire (616 B.C.) — Nineveh destroyed by Chaldeans (Neo-Babylonians) and Medes (612 B.C.). Founding of Byzantium by Greeks (c. 660 B.C.). Building of the Acropolis in Athens. Solon, Greek lawgiver (640–560 B.C.). Sappho of Lesbos, Greek poet (fl. c. 610–580 B.C.). Lao-tse, Chinese philosopher and founder of Taoism (born c. 604 B.C.).

600–500 B.C.

Babylonian King Nebuchadnezzar builds empire, destroys Jerusalem (586 B.C.). Babylonian Captivity of the Jews (starting 587 B.C.). Hanging Gardens of Babylon. Cyrus the Great of Persia creates great empire, conquers Babylon (539 B.C.), frees the Jews. Athenian democracy develops. Aeschylus, Greek dramatist (525–465 B.C.). Pythagoras, Greek philosopher and mathematician (582?–507? B.C.). Confucius (551–479 B.C.) develops ethical and social philosophy in China.

The *Analects* or Lun-yü ("collected sayings") are compiled by the
second generation of Confucian disciples. Buddha (563?–
483? B.C.) founds Buddhism in India.

500–400 B.C.

Greeks defeat Persians: battles of
Marathon (490 B.C.), Thermopylae (480 B.C.), Salamis (480 B.C.).
Peloponnesian Wars between Athens and Sparta (431–404 B.C.) —
Sparta victorious. Pericles comes to power in
Athens (462 B.C.). Flowering of Greek culture during the Age of
Pericles (450–400 B.C.). The Parthenon is built in Athens as a
temple of the goddess Athena (447–432 B.C.). Ictinus and
Callicrates are the architects and Phidias is responsible for the
sculpture. Sophocles, Greek dramatist (496?–
406 B.C.). Hippocrates, Greek "Father of Medicine"
(born 460 B.C.). Xerxes I, king of Persia (rules 485–465 B.C.).

400–300 B.C.

Pentateuch — first five books of the Old Testament evolve in final
form. Philip of Macedon, who believed himself to be a descendant
of the Greek people, assassinated (336 B.C.) after subduing the
Greek city-states; succeeded by son, Alexander the Great (356–
323 B.C.), who destroys Thebes (335 B.C.), conquers Tyre and
Jerusalem (332 B.C.), occupies Babylon (330 B.C.), invades India,
and dies in Babylon. His empire is divided among his generals;
one of them, Seleucis I, establishes Middle East empire with
capitals at Antioch (Syria) and Seleucia (in Iraq). Trial and
execution of Greek philosopher Socrates (399 B.C.). Dialogues
recorded by his student, Plato (c. 427–348 or 347 B.C.). Euclid's

work on geometry (323 B.C.). Aristotle, Greek philosopher (384–322 B.C.). Demosthenes, Greek orator (384–322 B.C.).Praxiteles, Greek sculptor (400–330 B.C.).

Did these angels, these gods create us and then come back to fine-tune their work or did they re-write the DNA of the humans here to give them the results they wanted?

There are stories in ancient Scripture naming the Angels or gods who created various portions of the human body. The engineering or creation could have been done on a genetic level. Each angel or God would have been in charge of the creation of various strands of genetic material resulting in limbs organs and attributes of the human body.

From "The Apocryphon of John" we read:
And a voice called from the highest kingdom of heaven: "The Man exists and the son of Man." And the head Archon, Yaldaboth, heard it and thought that the voice had come from his mother. He did not know whence it came. He taught them, the holy and perfect Mother-Father, the complete Foreknowledge, the image of the invisible one who is the Father of the all things and through whom everything came into being, the first Man. He is the one who revealed his image in human form.

And the whole kingdom of the first (head) Archon quaked, and

the foundations of the abyss shook. And the underside of waters, which are above the material world, were illuminated by the appearance of his image which had been revealed. When all the authorities and the head Archon looked, they saw the whole region of the underside (of the waters) that was illuminated. And through the light they saw the form of the image (reflected) in the water.

And he (Yaldaboth) said to the authorities of him, "Come, let us make a man using the image of God as a template to our likeness, that his image may become a light for us." And they created by the means of their various powers matching the features which were given to them. And each authority supplied a feature in the form of the image which Yaldaboth had seen in its natural form. He created a being according to the likeness of the first, perfect Man. And they said, "Let us call him Adam (man), that his name may be a power of light for us."

And the powers began to create.
The first one, Goodness, created a bone essence; and the second, Foreknowledge, created a sinew essence; the third, Divinity, created a flesh essence; and the fourth, the Lordship, created a marrow essence; the fifth, Kingdom created a blood essence; the sixth, Envy, created a skin essence; the seventh, Understanding, created a hair essence. And the multitude of the angels were with him and they received from the powers the seven elements of the natural (form) so they could create the proportions of the

limbs and the proportion of the buttocks and correct
functioning of each of the parts together.

The first one began to create the head. Eteraphaope-Abron
created his head; Meniggesstroeth created the brain; Asterechme
created the right eye; Thaspomocha, the left eye; Yeronumos, the
right ear; Bissoum, the left ear; Akioreim, the nose; Banen-
Ephroum, the lips; Amen, the teeth; Ibikan, the molars;
Basiliademe, the tonsils; Achcha, the uvula; Adaban, the neck;
Chaaman, the vertebrae; Dearcho, the throat; Tebar, the right
shoulder; the left shoulder; Mniarcon, the right elbow; the left
elbow; Abitrion, the right underarm; Evanthen, the left
underarm; Krys, the right hand; Beluai, the left hand; Treneu,
the fingers of the right hand; Balbel, the fingers of the left hand;
Kriman, the nails of the hands; Astrops, the right breast;
Barroph, the left breast; Baoum, the right shoulder joint; Ararim,
the left shoulder joint; Areche, the belly; Phthave, the navel;
Senaphim, the abdomen; Arachethopi, the right ribs; Zabedo,
the left ribs; Barias, the right hip; Phnouth the left hip;
Abenlenarchei, the marrow; Chnoumeninorin, the bones;
Gesole, the stomach; Agromauna, the heart; Bano, the lungs;
Sostrapal, the liver; Anesimalar, the spleen; Thopithro, the
intestines; Biblo, the kidneys; Roeror, the sinews; Taphreo, the
spine of the body; Ipouspoboba, the veins; Bineborin, the
arteries; Atoimenpsephei, theirs are the breaths which are in all
the limbs; Entholleia, all the flesh; Bedouk, the right buttock;
Arabeei, the penis; Eilo, the testicles; Sorma, the genitals;

Gorma-Kaiochlabar, the right thigh; Nebrith, the left thigh; Pserem, the kidneys of the right leg; Asaklas, the left kidney; Ormaoth, the right leg; Emenun, the left leg; Knyx, the right shin-bone; Tupelon, the left shin-bone; Achiel, the right knee; Phnene, the left knee; Phiouthrom, the right foot; Boabel, its toes; Trachoun, the left foot; Phikna, its toes; Miamai, the nails of the feet; Labernioum.

And those who were appointed over all of these are: Zathoth, Armas, Kalila, Jabel, (Sabaoth, Cain, Abel). And those who are particularly active in the limbs are the head Diolimodraza, the neck Yammeax, the right shoulder Yakouib, the left shoulder Verton, the right hand Oudidi, the left one Arbao, the fingers of the right hand Lampno, the fingers of the left hand Leekaphar, the right breast Barbar, the left breast Imae, the chest Pisandriaptes, the right shoulder joint Koade, the left shoulder joint Odeor, the right ribs Asphixix, the left ribs Synogchouta, the belly Arouph, the womb Sabalo, the right thigh Charcharb, the left thigh Chthaon, all the genitals Bathinoth, the right leg Choux, the left leg Charcha, the right shin-bone Aroer, the left shin-bone Toechtha, the right knee Aol, the left knee Charaner, the right foot Bastan, its toes Archentechtha, the left foot Marephnounth, its toes Abrana.

Seven have power over all of these: Michael, Ouriel, Asmenedas, Saphasatoel, Aarmouriam, Richram, Amiorps. And the ones who are in charge of the senses are Archendekta; and he who is in charge of the receptions is Deitharbathas; and he who is in charge over the imagination is Oummaa; and he who is over creativity Aachiaram, and he who is over the whole impulse Riaramnacho.

Could this be those constructing human DNA or the blueprint to the human form? Were we created as an experiment of another race?

Documents, much older than Christianity itself laid charges on the Angels of antiquity for manipulating the DNA of man and animals contrary to the wishes of their higher authority or commander. The result of the errant experiments of mixing alien DNA with human DNA were the three species mentioned in the Book of Jubilees. The Book of Enoch, also called First Enoch, and the Book of Jubilees begin the story of the Watchers. These books, The Book of Enoch and The Book of Jubilees, are considered canon by the Ethiopic Christian Church, one of the oldest sects of Christianity. Let us take a brief overview of these two books.

The Book of Enoch:

Of all the books quoted, paraphrased, or referred to in the Bible, the Book of Enoch has influenced the writers of the Bible as few others have. Even more extensively than in the Old Testament, the writers of the New Testament were frequently influenced by other writings, including the Book of Enoch.

It is not the purpose of this work to make judgments as to the validity or worth of the Book of Enoch, but rather to simply put forth a meaningful question. Is not the non-canonical book that most influenced the thought and theology of the writers of the New Testament worth further research and contemplation?

Before we continue in our study of the Book of Enoch there are several questions we must keep in mind. If a book is mentioned or quoted in the Bible is it not worthy of further study? If it is worth investigating, is this the book of which the Bible speaks? What knowledge or insight does it add to our understanding of the Bible or the men who wrote it?

The Book of Enoch was once cherished by Jews and Christians alike. It is read in certain Coptic Christian Churches in Ethiopia. Three versions of the Book of Enoch exist today.

Most scholars date the Book of Enoch, also called 1 Enoch, to sometime during the second century B.C. We do not know what earlier oral tradition, if any, the book contains. Enoch was considered inspired and authentic by certain Jewish sects of the first century B.C. and remained popular for at least five hundred years. The earliest Ethiopian text was apparently derived from a Greek manuscript of the Book of Enoch, which itself was a copy of an earlier text. The original was apparently written in the Semitic language, now thought to be Aramaic.

The Book of Enoch (1 Enoch) was discovered in the 18th century. It was assumed to have been penned after the beginning of the Christian era. This theory was based on the fact that it had quotes and paraphrases as well as concepts found in the New Testament. Thus, it was assumed that it was heavily influenced by writers such as Jude and Peter.

However, recent discoveries of copies of the book among the Dead Sea Scrolls found at Qumran prove the book was in existence before the time of Jesus Christ. These scrolls forced a closer look and reconsideration. It became obvious that the New Testament did not influence the Book of Enoch; on the contrary, the Book of Enoch influenced the New Testament. The date of the original writing upon which the second century B.C. Qumran copies were based is shrouded in obscurity. Likewise lost are the sources of the oral traditions that came to be the Book of Enoch. Slowly, over the past sixty years, we have unraveled some of the mystery.

The first century Christians accepted the Book of Enoch as inspired, if not authentic. They relied on it to understand the origin and purpose of many things, from angels to wind, sun, and stars. In fact, many of the key concepts used by Jesus Christ himself seem directly connected to terms and ideas in the Book of Enoch.

The theories regarding the authenticity of Enoch vary widely. Some believe Enoch is an elaboration on a biblical story. In this case it is suggested that Enoch expands Genesis chapter 6.

Another, more controversial theory has Enoch predating the Genesis story. Like the Book of Enoch, Genesis seems to have several authors with stories intertwined. One of these authors is known simply as "P" owing to the fact he was thought to be a priest. If we compare the "P" contribution of Genesis to the Book of Enoch parallels leap out.

Enoch   P

Corrupt earth   Human way corrupt on the earth (Gen 6)
eating animals   eating animals (Gen 9)
bloodshed   bloodshed (Gen 9)
364-day year   30-day months (Gen 7)
(12 months x 30 + 4)   365-day year (Gen 5)
Enoch goes to heaven   Enoch goes to heaven (Gen 5)

There are other connections. The name "Azazel" appears in Leviticus. The scapegoat is sent into the wilderness "to Azazel" and through the ceremony of laying on of hand by the priest and people the goat is sent away, bearing the sins of the people. This reference only makes sense if the writer believed that Azazel was responsible for all human sins and would bear the punishment for it, as the Book of Enoch declares.

In Genesis, it is Cain that bares sins into the wilderness. However, we will see that there are connections between the fallen angels and the descendants of Cain.

The problem with such a connection between The Book of Enoch and Genesis is that it does not point to the direction of the transmission.

It is hard to avoid the evidence that Jesus not only studied the book, but also respected it highly enough to allude to its doctrine and content. Other evidence of the early Christians' acceptance of the Book of Enoch was for many years buried under the King James Bible's mistranslation of Luke 9:35, describing the transfiguration of Christ: "And there came a voice out of the cloud, saying, 'This is my beloved Son. Hear him.' " Apparently the translator here wished to make this verse agree with a similar verse in Matthew and Mark. But

Luke's verse in the original Greek reads: "This is my Son, the Elect One (from the Greek ho eklelegmenos, lit., "the elect one"). Hear him."

The "Elect One" is a most significant term (found fourteen times) in the Book of Enoch. If the book was indeed known to the apostles of Christ, with its abundant descriptions of the Elect One who should "sit upon the throne of glory" and the Elect One who should "dwell in the midst of them;" then the great scriptural authenticity is justly accorded to the Book of Enoch when the "voice out of the cloud" tells the apostles, "This is my Son, the Elect One,"... the one promised in the Book of Enoch.

The Book of Jude tells us in Verse 14 that "Enoch, the seventh from Adam, prophesied." Jude also, in Verse 15, makes a direct reference to the Book of Enoch (2:1), where he writes, "to execute judgment on all, to convict all who are ungodly." As a matter of fact, it is a direct, word for word quote. Therefore, Jude's reference to the Enochian prophesies strongly leans toward the conclusion that these written prophesies were available to him at that time.

Fragments of ten Enoch manuscripts were found among the Dead Sea Scrolls. The number of scrolls indicate the Essenes (a Jewish commune or sect at the time of Christ) could well have used the Enochian writings as a community prayer book or teacher's manual and study text.

Many of the early church fathers also supported the Enochian writings. Justin Martyr ascribed all evil to demons whom he alleged to be the offspring of the angels who fell through lust for women; directly referencing the Enochian writings.

Athenagoras (170 A.D.), regarded Enoch as a true prophet. He describes the angels who "violated both their own nature and their office." In his writings, he goes into detail about the nature of fallen angels and the cause of their fall, which comes directly from the Enochian writings.

Irenaeus (A.D. 180) In his work "Against Heresies," spoke of Enoch, whose translation was a prophetic view of our future rapture: "For Enoch, when he pleased God, was translated in the same body in which he did please Him, thus pointing out by anticipation the translation of the just" (Against Heresies, bk. 5).

Since any book stands to be interpreted in many ways, Enoch posed problems for some theologians. Instead of reexamining their own theology, they sought to dispose of that which went counter to their beliefs. Some of the visions in Enoch are believed to point to the consummation of the age in conjunction with Christ's second coming which took place in A.D. 70 (in the destruction of Jerusalem).

This being the case, it should not surprise us that Enoch was declared a fake and was rejected by Hilary, Jerome, and Augustine. Enoch was subsequently lost to Western Christendom for over a thousand years.

However, some view the book of Enoch as prophetic, not only as a time line, but being a picture into what is coming to all those who believe and are obedient to God.

"By faith Enoch was translated that he should not see death; and was not found, because God had translated him: for before his translation he had this testimony, that he pleased God" (Hebrews 11:5). Enoch experienced "rapture" in his time before the judgment of the Flood. What Enoch experienced is what some modern Christians believe is waiting for the church. 1 Thes. 4:15-17 promises that Jesus will descend from heaven with a shout, with the voice of the archangel and the trumpet of God and the church will be taken up, or "raptured", to meet Him in the air. The Book of Enoch may inform and prepare us for coming events. Some believe there are prophecies contained in the Book of Enoch that are as applicable as those written in the books of Daniel and Revelation.

The prophecies within Enoch are presented in several ways. There is a list of weeks, much like those of Daniel. There are a list of animals and their actions toward each other. There is a list of generations defining a timeline.

Enoch's "seventy generations" was also a great problem. Many scholars thought it could not be made to stretch beyond the First Century. Copies of Enoch soon disappeared. Indeed, for almost two thousand years we knew only the references made to it in the Bible. Without having the book itself, we could not have known it was being quoted in the Bible, sometimes word for word by Peter and Jude.

"...the Lord, having saved a people out of the land of Egypt, afterward destroyed them that believed not. And angels that kept not their own principality, but left their proper habitation, he hath kept in everlasting bonds under darkness unto the judgment of the great day. Even as Sodom and Gomorrah, and the cities about them...in like manner...are set out as examples...." (Jude 5-7)

"For if God spared not the angels when they sinned, but cast them down into hell, and committed them to pits of darkness, to be reserved unto judgment." (2 Peter 2.4)

To what extent other New Testament writers regarded Enoch as scriptural canon may be determined by comparing their writings with those found in Enoch. A strong possibility of influence upon their thought and choice of wording is evidenced by a great many references found in Enoch which remind one of passages found in the New Testament.

Enoch was also referenced in other writings, such as the Book of Jubilees, which is canon in the Ethiopic Christian Church, and the Book of Giant, in which one of the fallen angels is called by the name of Gilgamesh.

The Book of Enoch seems to be a missing link between Jewish and Christian theology and is considered by many to be more Christian in its theology than Jewish. It was considered scripture by many early Christians. The literature of the church fathers is filled with references to this book. The early second century apocryphal book of the Epistle of Barnabus makes many references and quotes from the Book of Enoch. Second and third century church fathers like Justin Martyr, Irenaeus, Origin and Clement of Alexandria all seemed to have accepted Enoch as authentic. Tertullian (160-230 A.D.) even called the Book of Enoch, "Holy Scripture". The Ethiopian Coptic Church holds the Book of Enoch as part of its official spiritual canon. It was widely known and read the first three centuries after Christ. This and many other books became discredited after the Council of Laodicea. And being under ban of the authorities, it gradually disappeared from circulation.

In 1773, rumors of a surviving copy of the book drew Scottish explorer James Bruce to distant Ethiopia. He found the Book of Enoch had been preserved by the Ethiopian church, which put it right alongside the other books of the Bible.

Bruce secured not one, but three Ethiopian copies of the book and brought them back to Europe and Britain. In 1773 Bruce returned from six years in Abyssinia. In 1821 Richard Laurence published the first English translation. The famous R.H. Charles edition was published in 1912.

In the following years several portions of the Greek text surfaced. Then with the discovery of cave 4 at Qumran, seven fragmentary copies of the Aramaic text were discovered. This means the text passed from its Aramaic form into Greek, and finally into Geez, an Ethiopian tongue.

Before the discovery of the Aramaic form was uncovered, it was thought that Enoch was written after Jude and borrowed heavily from it. However, after the discovery of Enoch among the texts in Qumran, scholars had to re-examine the evidence. Enoch not only existed long before the biblical book of Jude, it is now obvious that both Jude and Peter read, believed and borrowed heavily from Enoch. This makes the Book of Enoch (1 Enoch) one of the earliest apocalyptic books.

Most apocalyptic literature was written after the destruction of the Jewish temple in Jerusalem in 70 A.D. under the feet of a Roman siege. Rome was considered by the Jews to be an ungodly nation as well as the oppressors and enemy of the Jews. The Jews considered themselves to be the chosen people of God. When the temple of God was destroyed it caused great turmoil throughout Judaism. Why would God let this happen to His chosen people and moreover, to His own house? The answer must be that the Jewish people had sinned and wondered away from the will of God. If this were true then when the Jewish nation repented and came back to God, He would avenge them by allowing the Jews to conquer and crush their enemies. The Jews would once again appear to be the victorious and chosen people their were meant to be. The return of the Jewish nation to the strict will and law of God and the battle and victory through God's help is the basis of most apocalyptic literature.

This is not the case in the first and oldest section of the Book of Enoch, written as early as the 3rd century B.C. The apocalyptic theme in the section we are calling "The Book of the Watchers" is a simple one of blessing the righteous and destroying the unrighteous beings, both human and angelic. More traditional or common apocalyptic themes can be seen in sections of Enoch written around 100 A.D.

The Book of Enoch is not one manuscript. It is a composite of several manuscripts written by several authors over a period of three to four hundred years.

The Book of Enoch is composed of six main parts. These sections can be subdivided further. It could be argued that, like the writers of the Bible itself, the various authors of Enoch did not foresee their contributions being concatenated into a single volume. The six basic sections are as follows:

The *Book of Watchers* (Chapters 1-36):
Late third century or early second century B.C. Overall theme - Last   Judgment. This section is considered to be the most authentic and important part of the Book of Enoch.
Introduction (Chapters 1-5): Last Judgment;
The Fall (Chapters 6-36): Fall of the angels by having sex with the women of earth. The evil of the children and the corruption of

mankind.

The *Book of Parables* (Chapters 37-71):

First century A.D. Overall theme – The Messiah and his Judgment.

First parable: Enoch's vision on heaven containing the righteous   people, the angels and the Messiah. (Chapters 38-44);

Second parable: The messianic judgment. (Chapters 45-57)

Third parable: The Son of Man (Chapters 58-71).

The Book of *Astronomy and Calendar* (Chapters 72-82):

Late third or early second century B.C. Overall theme – Elements of weather, movement of stars, planets, sun and moon, and the calendar.

The *Book of Visions* (Chapters 83-90):

165-160 B.C. (Thought to be written around the time of the revolt led by the Maccabees.) Overall theme – Judgment and history.

First vision: the Deluge as the first judgment (Chapters 83-84);

Second vision: a history of Israel until the revolt (Chapters 85-90).

The *Book of Warnings and Blessings of Enoch* (Chapters 91-104):

Early second century B.C. Overall theme - Warnings, blessings and an apocalypse.

The prophecy of the Apocalypse of Weeks. (Chapters 91 and 93)

What will befall sinners and the righteous. (Chapters 94-104)

Later Additions to the Text – Book of Noah **(Chapters 105-108):**

Second century B.C. Overall theme - Noah and Methuselah.

This section of the book seems to be added as an afterthought. It consists of fragments from other books, such as the Book of Noah.

When the Book of Enoch was found along with other scrolls around the Dead Sea, the Book of Parables was not included. This was because that section was added later. In addition, the Book of Watchers and the Book of Visions were already joined and intact.

It is the Book of the Watchers that will most concern us in our study. The Book of Enoch, as well as the Book of Jubilees, are available from Fifth Estate Publishing.

The Book of Jubilees:

Scholars believe Jubilees was composed in the second century B.C. The Hebrew fragments found at Qumran are part of a Jewish library that contained other supporting literature such as the Book of Enoch and others. An analysis of the chronological development in the shapes of letters in the manuscripts confirms that Jubilees is pre-Christian in date and seems to have been penned between 100 and 200 B.C. Based on records of the High Priests of the time, the date of authorship is probably 140 – 100 B.C. The book of Jubilees is also cited in the Qumran Damascus Document in pre-Christian texts.

The Book of Jubilees was originally written in Hebrew. The author was a Pharisee (a doctor of the law), or someone very familiar with scripture and religious law. Since the scrolls were found in what is assumed to be an Essene library, and were dated to the time the Essene community was active, the author was probably a member of that particular religious group.

Time within the book is broken down into Jubilees, which are sections of 50 years each. Jubilees, Chapter 7 reveals the horror and unintended consequences brought upon the earth by the Watchers when they impregnated women of the earth and mixed alien DNA with human DNA.

When the Book of Enoch is placed with the Book of Jubilees, and the story is compared to the Bible the descent and violations of the Watchers upon the earth comes into sharp focus and the existent of their interference is seen.

Enoch **[Chapter 6]**
1 And it came to pass when the children of men had multiplied

that in those days were born to them beautiful and fair daughters.

GEN 6:1 And it came to pass, when men began to multiply on the face of the earth, and daughters were born unto them, 2 That the sons of God saw the daughters of men that they were fair; and they took them wives of all which they chose. 3 And the LORD said, My spirit shall not always strive with man, for that he also is flesh: yet his days shall be an hundred and twenty years.

2 And the angels, the sons of heaven, saw and lusted after them, and said to one another: 'Come, let us choose us wives from among the children of men

3 And have children with them.' And Semjaza, who was their leader, said to them: 'I fear you will not agree to do this deed,

4 And I alone shall have to pay the penalty of this great sin.'

5 And they all answered him and said: 'Let us all swear an oath, and all bind ourselves by mutual curses so we will not abandon this plan but to do this thing.' Then they all swore together and bound themselves by mutual curses.

6 And they were in all two hundred who descended in the days of Jared in the summit of Mount Hermon, and they called it

Mount Hermon, because they had sworn and bound themselves by mutual curses on the act.

JUD 1:5 *I will therefore put you in remembrance, though ye once knew this, how that the Lord, having saved the people out of the land of Egypt, afterward destroyed them that believed not. 6 And the angels who kept not their first estate, but left their own habitation, he hath reserved in everlasting chains under darkness unto the judgment of the great day.*

7 And these are the names of their leaders: Samlazaz, their leader, Araklba, Rameel, Kokablel, Tamlel, Ramlel, Danel, Ezeqeel, Baraqijal,

(Author's note: Samlazaz could be another spelling of Semjaza, and possibly be the same entity.)

8 Asael, Armaros, Batarel, Ananel, Zaqiel, Samsapeel, Satarel, Turel, Jomjael, Sariel. These are their chiefs of tens.

[Chapter 7]

1 And all of them together went and took wives for themselves, each choosing one for himself, and they began to go in to them and to defile themselves with sex with them,

GEN 5:32 And Noah was five hundred years old: and Noah begat Shem, Ham, and Japheth. 6:1 And it came to pass, when men began to multiply on the face of the earth, and daughters were born unto them, 2 That the sons of God saw the daughters of men that they were fair; and they took them wives of all which they chose. 3 And the LORD said, My spirit shall not always strive with man, for that he also is flesh: yet his days shall be an hundred and twenty years. 4 There were giants in the earth in those days; and also after that, when the sons of God came in unto the daughters of men, and they bare children to them, the same became mighty men which were of old, men of renown. 5 And GOD saw that the wickedness of man was great in the earth, and that every imagination of the thoughts of his heart was only evil continually. 6 And it repented the LORD that he had made man on the earth, and it grieved him at his heart.

2 And the angels taught them charms and spells, and the cutting of roots, and made them acquainted with plants.

3 And the women became pregnant, and they bare large giants, whose height was three thousand cubits (ells).

Jubilees 7
21 Because of these three things came the flood on the earth, namely, the fornication that the Watchers committed against the law of their ordinances when they went whoring after the daughters of men, and took themselves wives of all they chose, and they made the beginning of

uncleanness.

22 And they begat sons, the Naphilim (Naphidim), and they were all dissimilar, and they devoured one another, and the Giants killed the Naphil, and the Naphil killed the Eljo, and the Eljo killed mankind, and one man killed one another.

23 Every one committed himself to crime and injustice and to shed much blood, and the earth was filled with sin.

24 After this they sinned against the beasts and birds, and all that moved and walked on the earth, and much blood was shed on the earth, and men continually desired only what was useless and evil.

25 And the Lord destroyed everything from the face of the earth. Because of the wickedness of their deeds, and because of the blood they had shed over all the earth, He destroyed everything. "

4 The giants consumed all the work and toil of men. And when men could no longer sustain them, the giants turned against them and devoured mankind.

5 And they began to sin against birds, and beasts, and reptiles, and fish, and to devour one another's flesh, and drank the blood.

6 Then the earth laid accusation against the lawless ones.

Jasher 2

19 For in those days the sons of men began to trespass against God, and to go contrary to the commandments which he had given Adam, to be prolific and reproduce in the earth.

20 And some of the sons of men caused their wives to drink a mixture that would render them unable to conceive, in order that they might retain their figures and their beautiful appearance might not fade.

21 And when the sons of men caused some of their wives to drink, Zillah drank with them.

22 And the child-bearing women appeared abominable in the sight of their husbands and they treated them as widows, while their husbands lived with those unable to conceive and to those women they were attached.

Genesis 4:8 And Cain talked with Abel his brother: and it came to pass, when they were in the field, that Cain rose up against Abel his brother, and slew him. 9And the LORD said unto Cain, Where is Abel thy brother? And he said, I know not: Am I my brother's keeper? 10And he said, What hast thou done? the voice of thy brother's blood crieth unto me from the ground. 11And now art thou cursed from the earth, which hath opened her mouth to receive thy brother's blood from thy hand; 12When thou tillest the ground, it shall not henceforth yield unto thee her strength; a fugitive and a vagabond shalt thou be in the earth.

[Chapter 8]

1 And Azazel taught men to make swords, and knives, and shields, and breastplates, and taught them about metals of the

earth and the art of working them, and bracelets, and ornaments, and the use of antimony, and the beautifying of the eyelids, and all kinds of precious stones, and all coloring and dyes.

2 And there was great impiety, they turned away from God, and committed fornication, and they were led astray, and became corrupt in all their ways.

Matthew 5:19 (New International Version)
19Anyone who breaks one of the least of these commandments and teaches others to do the same will be called least in the kingdom of heaven, but whoever practices and teaches these commands will be called great in the kingdom of heaven.

3 Semjaza taught the casting of spells, and root-cuttings, Armaros taught counter-spells (release from spells), Baraqijal taught astrology, Kokabel taught the constellations (portents), Ezeqeel the knowledge of the clouds, Araqiel the signs of the earth, Shamsiel the signs of the sun, and Sariel the course of the moon. And as men perished, they cried, and their cry went up to heaven.

Jasher 4
18 And their judges and rulers went to the daughters of men and took their wives by force from their husbands according to their choice, and the sons of men in those days took from the cattle of the earth, the beasts

of the field and the fowls of the air, and taught the mixture of animals of one species with the other, in order therewith to provoke the Lord; and God saw the whole earth and it was corrupt, for all flesh had corrupted its ways on earth, all men and all animals.

19 And the Lord said, I will blot out man that I created from the face of the earth, yea from man to the birds of the air together with cattle and beasts that are in the field for I repent that I made them.

20 And all men who walked in the ways of the Lord died in those days, before the Lord brought the evil on man which he had declared, for this was from the Lord that they should not see the evil which the Lord spoke of concerning the sons of men.

Jubilees Chapter 7:20 In the twenty-eighth jubilee Noah began to direct his sons in the ordinances and commandments, and all the judgments that he knew, and he exhorted his sons to observe righteousness, and to cover the shame of their flesh, and to bless their Creator, and honor father and mother, and love their neighbor, and guard their souls from fornication and uncleanness and all iniquity.

21 Because of these three things came the flood on the earth, namely, the fornication that the Watchers committed against the law of their ordinances when they went whoring after the daughters of men, and took themselves wives of all they chose, and they made the beginning of uncleanness.

22 And they begat sons, the naphilim (Naphidim), and they were all dissimilar, and they devoured one another, and the Giants killed the Naphil, and the Naphil killed the Eljo, and the Eljo killed mankind, and one man killed one another.

23 Every one committed himself to crime and injustice and to shed much blood, and the earth was filled with sin.

24 After this they sinned against the beasts and birds, and all that moved and walked on the earth, and much blood was shed on the earth, and men continually desired only what was useless and evil.

25 And the Lord destroyed everything from the face of the earth. Because of the wickedness of their deeds, and because of the blood they had shed over all the earth, He destroyed everything. "

26 We were left, I and you, my sons, and everything that entered with us into the ark, and behold I see your works before me that you do not walk in righteousness, for in the path of destruction you have begun to walk, and you are turning one against another, and are envious one of another, and so it comes that you are not in harmony, my sons, each with his brother.

27 For I see the demons have begun their seductions against you and against your children and now I fear on your behalf, that after my death you will shed the blood of men on the earth, and that you, too, will be destroyed from the face of the earth.

Are the stories in Ancient literature actually breadcrumbs left behind, which point back to the beginning of the creation of mankind by beings called Gods? In the first book of Enoch we are told the watchers, who were a race of Angels, were given the chore of monitoring mankind in order to record their deeds, actions, and activity. These beings, according to other ancient Scriptures, came to earth, thus violating their prime directive of non-interference, and altered the evolution and course of mankind by interbreeding with the women at that time. Was this an example of the creator falling in love with his creation? The Watchers placed foreign, angelic, DNA in the bloodline of mankind. The resulting offspring or Giants, monsters, and a race called the Eljo or Elyo. These hybrids were the men of legend, the monsters of mythology, and the Giants who roamed the earth. The actions of the Angels negated the experiment, which was saved by eliminating the results of their mistakes, leaving one single uncontaminated genetic lineage to survive the flood and continue the experiment.

The story is repeated over and over in a line of legends and scriptures spanning thousands of years. Other scriptures, such as the book of Jasher has within it the same narrative of destruction. The Book of Giants, a recently discovered document recording the thoughts and dreams of the Watchers themselves reveals the identical scenario from the angelic or demonic perspective.

From the Book of Jasher it is reported the angels disregarded the wishes of their commander and violated the experiment, producing monsters.

The Mormon Church, otherwise known as The Church of Jesus

Christ of Latter-day Saints, considers Jasher to be the book referenced in the Old Testament. The belief of the church leadership is bolstered by the preface in the 1625 version, which claims its original source came from the ruins of Jerusalem in 70 A.D.

Jasher is held in high repute by many Mormons but is not officially endorsed by the Mormon Church. The official stance of the Mormon Church falls short of making Jasher part of their Holy Scriptures but does endorse the book as being valid and authentic.

The Mormon Church places the book of Jasher on the same level as other apocryphal writings.

Jasher 4: 18 And their judges and rulers (the Watchers) went to the daughters of men and took their wives by force from their husbands according to their choice, and the sons of men (The Watchers) in those days took from the cattle of the earth, the beasts of the field and the fowls of the air, and taught the mixture of animals of one species with the other, in order therewith to provoke the Lord; and God (El) saw the whole earth and it was corrupt, for all flesh had corrupted its ways on earth, all men and all animals.

19 And the Lord said, I will blot out man that I created from the face of the earth, yea from man to the birds of the air together with cattle and beasts that are in the field, for I repent that I made them.

20 All men who walked in the ways of the Lord died in those days, before the Lord brought the evil on man which he had declared, for this was from the Lord that they should not see the evil which the Lord spoke of concerning the sons of men.

21 And Noah found grace in the sight of the Lord, and the Lord chose him and his children to raise up offspring on the face of the whole earth.

It is here the story takes an unexpected turn, for when the Watchers understood the extent of their transgression and the anger of El they began to beg forgiveness and plead to come back home. The story of the nightmares and dread of the Watchers is documented in the Book of Giants.

The manuscript of the Giants is broken and fragmented. Much of its contents remain a matter of guesswork. Indeed, to make sense of some of the manuscript words or phrases had to be inserted on a "best guess" bais. These words, which are missing from the original fragmented text, are placed within square brackets [].

 Most of the content of the present fragments concern dreams regarding the giants and Enoch's attempt to interpret them. Little more than dust remains of the part of the text concerning the giants. Based on the fact that the name of one of the giants is Gilgamesh we can assume that there was some "crosspollination" between The Book of Giants and the ancient Near Eastern mythic epic. The name of one of the angels being the same as the Babylonian god-king and hero adds weight to the theory that the titans, heroes, and demigods of old are the fallen angels or their offspring. One must decide whether the epic story influenced this Book of Giants or if the Watchers were in fact the men of renown, as the Bible states.

The dates of the separate documents and events only add to the confusion. The Babylonian epic was written in the third millennium B.C.E. To place the time of the flood one should note that fragments of the Babylonian flood story were found in excavations at Megiddo and dated to around the fourteenth century B.C.E. So the legend of the Great Flood was already established in the Middle East long before Gilgamesh, the Israelite kingdom, or the Bible.

1 [...]
2[. . .] they knew the secrets of [the angels]
3[and] sin was great in the earth [. . .]
4[and there were the Watchers] and they killed man [and took to themselves the daughters of men] 5[. . . they begat] giants [. . .] The angels exploit (consumed) the fruits (fruitfulness) of the earth (consumed all the foods of the earth.)

[... and everything that the] earth produced [...] [...] the great fish [. . .]
14[. . .] the sky with all that grew [. . .] 15[. . . fruit of] the earth and all kinds of grain and all the trees [and their fruits.] 16[. . .] beasts and reptiles . . . [all creeping things of the earth and they observed all [uncleanness]

8[And they preformed every harsh deed and [blasphemous] utterance [. . .]

Emanuel Rapha

19[*and sexual deeds on*] *male and female, and among humans* [
and on animals.]

*Note: The two hundred angels chose animals on which to perform
unnatural acts on men, women, and animals.*

1 [. . . *two hundred*] 2 *donkeys, two hundred asses, two hundred* .
. . *rams of the*] 3 *flock, two hundred goats, two hundred* [. . . *beast
of the*] 4 *field from every animal, from every* [*bird* . . .] 5[. . .] *for
sexual acts regardless of species* [. . .] *The outcome of the
demonic corruption was violence, perversion, and a brood of
monstrous beings.*

[. . .] *they defiled* [*themselves*] 2[. . . *they begot*] *giants and
monsters* [. . .] 3[. . .] *they begot, and, behold, all* [*the earth was
corrupted* . . .] 4[. . .] *with its blood and by the hand of* [*the
angels. And there was sin and death committed by the offspring of
the angels, which are giants. .And the giants began to devour the
animals.*] 5[*giant's*] *which did not suffice for them and* [. . .] 6[. .
.] *and they were seeking to devour many* [*humans...*] 7[. . .] 8[
and when an animal was offered] *the monsters attacked it.*

2[*Monsters defiled all*] *flesh* [. . .] 3 *all* [. . .] *monsters* [. . .]
will be [. . .] 4[*There were offspring of the monsters and*] *they
would arise* [. . .] *lacking in true knowledge* [. . .] *because* [. . .]
5[. . .] *the earth* [*grew corrupt* . . .] *mighty* [. . .] 6[. . .] *they were
considering* [. . .] 7[. . .] *from the angels upon* [. . .] 8[. . .] *in the*

116

end it will perish and die [. . .] 9[. . .] they caused great corruption in the [earth . . .] [. . . this did not] suffice to [. . .] "they will be [. . .]

Note: The giants begin to be troubled by a series of dreams and visions. Mahway, the titan son of the angel Barakel, reports the first of these dreams to his fellow giants. He sees a tablet being immersed in water. When it emerges, all but three names have been washed away. The dream evidently symbolizes the destruction of all but Noah and his sons by the Flood.

[And one of the giants dreamed a dream...] they drenched the tablet in the water . . .] 2[. . .] the waters went up over the [tablet . . .] 3[. . .] they lifted out the tablet from the water of [. . .] The giant goes to the others and they discuss the dream.

1[. . . this vision] is for cursing and sorrow. I am the one who confessed 2[. . .] the whole group of the castaways that I shall go to [. . .] 3[. . . the spirits of the slain complaining about their killers and crying out 4[. . .] that we shall die together and be made an end of [. . .] much and I will be sleeping, and bread 6[. . .] for my dwelling; the vision and also [. . .] entered into the gathering of the giants 8[. . .]

1 [. . .] Ohya and he said to Mahway [. . .] 2[. . .] without trembling. Who showed you all this vision, [my] brother? 3[. . .] Barakel, my father, was with me. 4[. . .] Before Mahway had

*finished telling what [he had seen . . .] 5[. . . said] to him, Now I
have heard wonders! If a barren woman gives birth [. . .]*

*[the sons of Shemihaza were Ohya and Hahya.] 3[There] upon
Ohya said to Hahya . . .] 4[. . . to be destroyed] from upon the
earth and [. . .] 5[. . . the earth. When 6[. . .] they wept before
[the giants . . .]*

*3[. . .] your strength [. . .] 4[. . .] 5 Thereupon Ohya [said] to
Hahya [. . .] Then he answered, It is not for us, but for Azaiel, 6
for he did [. . . the children of] angels 7 are the giants, and they
would not let all their loved ones] be neglected [. . . we have] not
been cast down; you have strength [. . .]*

*3[. . .] I am a giant, and by the mighty strength of my arm and my
own great strength 4 [I can defeat] anyone mortal, and I have
made war against them; but I am not [strong enough for our
heavenly opponent or to be] able to stand against them, for my
opponents 6[. . .] reside in Heaven, and they dwell in the holy
places. And not 7[on the earth and they] are stronger than I. 8[. . .
] of the wild beast has come, and the wild man they call me. 9[. . .
] Then Ohya said to him, I have been forced to have a dream [. . .]
the sleep of my eyes vanished in order to let me see a vision. Now
I know that on [. . .] 11-12[. . .] Gilgamesh [. . .]*

*Note: The first speaker may be Gilgamesh. He has realized the
futility of warring against the forces of heaven.*

1 three of its roots [. . .] [while] I was [watching,] there came [. . . they moved the roots into] 3 this garden, all of them, and not [. . .]

Note: Ohya's dream vision is of a tree that is uprooted except for three of its roots; the vision's primary meaning is the same as that of the first dream.

1 concerns the death of our souls [. . .] and all his comrades, and Ohya told them what Gilgamesh said to him 2[. . .] and it was said [. . .] "concerning [. . .] the leader has cursed the authorities and rulers" 3 and the giants were glad at his words. Then he turned and left [. . .]

Note: Ohya tries to avoid the implications of the visions. Above he stated that it referred only to the demon Azazel; here he suggests that the destruction is for the earthly rulers alone.

4 and the sleep of their eye fled from them, and they arose and came to [. . . and told] their dreams, and said in the assembly of their peers, the monsters 6[. . . In] my dream I was watching this very night 7[and there was a garden, and in it were] gardeners and they were watering 8[. . . two hundred trees and] large shoots came out of their root 9[. . .] all the water, and the fire burned all 10[the garden . . .] They found the giants to tell them 11[the dream . . .]

Note: More dreams afflict the giants. The details of this vision are obscure, but it does not bode well for the giants. The dreamers speak first to the monsters, then to the giants. Two of them have had visions or dreams.

Note: Someone suggests that Enoch be found to interpret the vision.

[Go to Enoch,] the noted scribe, and he will interpret for us 12 the dream. Thereupon his fellow Ohya declared and said to the giants, 13 I too had a dream this night, O giants, and, behold, the Ruler of Heaven came down to earth 14[and destroyed all of us] and such is the end of the dream. [Thereupon] all the giants [and monsters] grew afraid 15 and called Mahway. He came to them and the giants pleaded with him and sent him to Enoch 16[the noted scribe]. They said to him, Go [. . .] to you that 17[. . .] you have heard his voice. And he said to him, He will [. . . and] interpret the dreams [. . .] [and he will tell you] how long the giants have to live. [. . .]

Note: After a journey through time and space, Mahway comes to Enoch and makes his request.

[. . . he soared up in the air] 4 like strong winds, and flew with his hands (flapping) like eagles . . . he left behind] 5 the inhabited world and passed over Desolation, the great desert [and he found

Enoch] 6 and Enoch saw him and hailed him, and Mahway said to him [and he yelled] 7 here and there a second time to Mahway [and Mahway said] . . . The giants await 8 your words, and all the monsters of the earth. If [. . .] has been carried [. . .] 9 from the days of [. . .] their [. . .] and they will be added [. . .] 10[regarding the dreams and visions,] we would know from you their meaning [. . .]11[In one of the visions] two hundred trees that from heaven [came down. . .]

1 three of its roots [. . .] [while] I was [watching,] there came [. . . they moved the roots into] 3 this garden, all of them, and not [. . .]

Note: Enoch sends back a tablet with its grim message of judgment, but with hope for repentance.

1 The scribe [Enoch . . .] 2[. . .] 3 a copy of the second tablet that Enoch sent [. . .] 4 in the very handwriting of Enoch the noted scribe [. . .] In the name of God the great 5 and holy one, to Shemihaza and all [his companions . . .] 6 let it be known to you that not [one of you will be left] 7 and the things you have done, and that your wives [. . .] 8 they and their sons and the wives of [their sons . . .] 9 by your licentiousness on the earth, and there has been upon you [. . . and the land is crying out] 10 and complaining about you and the deeds of your children [. . .] 11 the harm that you have done to it. [. . .] 12 until Raphael arrives, behold, destruction [is coming, in the form a great flood, and it will destroy all living things] 13 and whatever is in the deserts and the seas. And the meaning of the matter [is that judgement is] 14 upon you for evil. But now, loosen the bonds binding you to evil . [repent] 15 and pray.

Note: This fragment details a vision that Enoch saw.

3[. . . great fear] seized me and I fell on my face; I heard his voice [. . .] 4[. . .] he dwelt among human beings but he did not learn from them [. . .]

The Memory of Our DNA

Thus, we were made, DNA strand by DNA strand, until life became viable and man was created. It is not clear if life was introduced and allowed to evolve or if the evolution was overseen and the DNA manipulated. What is clear is the introduction of alien DNA into our gene pool was seen as a high crime, a crime so heinous and widespread that those most infected with the new DNA had to be eradicated, leaving only eight genetic lines to continue. Noah, his wife, his sons, and their wives were left to continue the experiment. The genetic code of these individuals were not totally error free, but had a smaller degree of error than the rest. They were within a degree of tolerance that could be controlled.

However, there was still genetic contamination and recessive traits from the alien DNA, which expressed itself at times. There were giants, who had six fingers on each hand and six toes on each foot. There were men who possessed remarkable abilities, there were the Nephilim, also translated as "the fallen ones" by some scholars and "giants" by other scholars. We will see later that some offspring lack a genetic code called, "the God gene," which was implanted within humans to facilitate obedience, and in all humans the God gene was weakened as it was overwritten by the DNA of angels or aliens.

Genesis 6

King James Version

1And it came to pass, when men began to multiply on the face of the earth, and daughters were born unto them, 2That the sons of God saw the daughters of men that they were fair; and they took them wives of all which they chose. 3And the LORD said, My spirit shall not always strive with man, for that he also is flesh: yet his days shall be an hundred and twenty years. 4There were giants in the earth in those days; and also after that, when the sons of God came in unto the daughters of men, and they bare children to them, the same became mighty men which were of old, men of renown.

5And GOD saw that the wickedness of man was great in the earth, and that every imagination of the thoughts of his heart was only evil continually. 6And it repented the LORD that he had made man on the earth, and it grieved him at his heart. 7And the LORD said, I will destroy man whom I have created from the face of the earth; both man, and beast, and the creeping thing, and the fowls of the air; for it repenteth me that I have made them. 8But Noah found grace in the eyes of the LORD.

9These are the generations of Noah: Noah was a just man and perfect in his generations, and Noah walked with God. 10And Noah begat three sons, Shem, Ham, and Japheth.

Here are other translations that may help explain the relationship between the mixture of DNA and the giants, heroes, and fallen ones.

New Living Translation (©2007)
In those days, and for some time after, giant Nephilites lived on the earth, for whenever the sons of God had intercourse with women, they gave birth to children who became the heroes and famous warriors of ancient times.

New American Standard Bible (©1995)
The Nephilim were on the earth in those days, and also afterward, when the sons of God came in to the daughters of men, and they bore children to them. Those were the mighty men who were of old, men of renown.

Holman Christian Standard Bible (©2009)
The Nephilim were on the earth both in those days and afterward, when the sons of God came to the daughters of mankind, who bore children to them. They were the powerful men of old, the famous men.

International Standard Version (©2012)
The Nephilim were on the earth at that time (and also immediately afterward), when those divine beings were having sexual relations with those human women, who gave birth to children for them. These children became the heroes and legendary figures of ancient times.

Giants show up later in battles against the Israelites. They all had six fingers and toes. This recessive trait may be a marker of alien ancestry.

1 Chronicles 20
New International Version 1984
The Capture of Rabbah

1In the spring, at the time when kings go off to war, Joab led out the armed forces. He laid waste the land of the Ammonites and went to Rabbah and besieged it, but David remained in Jerusalem. Joab attacked Rabbah and left it in ruins. 2David took the crown from the head of their kinga – its weight was found to be a talentb of gold, and it was set with precious stones – and it was placed on David's head. He took a great quantity of plunder from the city 3and brought out the people who were there, consigning them to labor with saws and with iron picks and axes. David did this to all the Ammonite towns. Then David and his entire army returned to Jerusalem.

War With the Philistines

4In the course of time, war broke out with the Philistines, at Gezer. At that time Sibbecai the Hushathite killed Sippai, one of the descendants of the Rephaites, and the Philistines were subjugated.

5In another battle with the Philistines, Elhanan son of Jair killed Lahmi the brother of Goliath the Gittite, who had a spear with a shaft like a weaver's rod.

6In still another battle, which took place at Gath, there was a huge man with six fingers on each hand and six toes on each foot — twenty-four in all. He also was descended from Rapha. 7When he taunted Israel, Jonathan son of Shimea, David's brother, killed him.

8These were descendants of Rapha in Gath, and they fell at the hands of David and his men.

Footnotes:
a 2 Or of Milcom, that is, Molech
b 2 That is, about 75 pounds (about 34 kilograms)

It appears, below, that Goliath had four brothers or that these four were the sons of Goliath:

2 Samuel 21:15-22

15 Moreover the Philistines had yet war again with Israel; and David went down, and his servants with him, and fought against the Philistines: and David waxed faint.
16 And Ishbibenob, which was of the sons of the giant, the weight of whose spear weighed three hundred shekels of brass in weight, he being girded with a new sword , thought to have slain David
17 But Abishai the son of Zeruiah succoured him, and smote the Philistine, and killed him. Then the men of David sware unto him, saying, Thou shalt go no more out with us to battle, that thou quench not the light of Israel.

18 And it came to pass after this, that there was again a battle with the Philistines at Gob: then Sibbechai the Hushathite slew Saph, which was of the sons of the giant.

19And there was again a battle in Gob with the Philistines, where Elhanan the son of Jaareoregim, a Bethlehemite, slew the brother of Goliath the Gittite, the staff of whose spear was like a weaver' beam.

20 And there was yet a battle in Gath, where was a man of great stature, that had on every hand six fingers, and on every foot six toes, four and twenty in number; and he also was born to the giant.

21 And when he defied Israel, Jonathan the son of Shimea the brother of David slew him.

22 These four were born to the giant in Gath, and fell by the hand of David, and by the hand of his servants.

What was the original intent of the DNA experiment and why was it important to keep the encoded DNA pure? The answer may come from a recent experiment, which has successfully encoded and read vast amounts of data into small volumes of DNA. Written in the DNA on this planet may be the sum and total knowledge of another civilization.

Excerpts from the magazine, "ScienceNews"
June 30, 2012
DNA used as rewritable data storage in cells.
Genetically encoded memory could track cell division inside the body.

Scientists in the UK have stored about a megabyte's worth of text, images and speech into a speck of DNA and then retrieved that data back almost faultlessly. They say that a larger-scale version of the technology could provide an extremely dense and long-lived form of digital storage that is particularly well suited to data archiving.

As ever-greater quantities of electronic data are produced, the problem of how to store that data becomes more acute. The hard disks and magnetic tape are expensive and need a source of electricity to read or write. These types of storage starts to degrade after a few years. Memory sticks like thumb drives are very limited in capacity at this time.

In the latest research, Nick Goldman and colleagues at the European Bioinformatics Institute near Cambridge have stored digital information by encoding it in the four different bases that make up DNA. While the storage technique does not offer the convenience of random access or being rewriteable, it does have a couple of major advantages. One is its extremely high density – as a result of the information being stored at the molecular level – and the other is its durability. As Goldman points out, intact DNA has been extracted from Neanderthal bones tens of thousands of years old. "Nature has discovered that this molecule is very stable," he says. "And we are piggy-backing on nature."

The group used DNA that was produced in the lab rather than

from inside living organisms, since the latter is vulnerable to mutation and hence data loss. Goldman and colleagues devised a coding scheme in which a fraction of each string is reserved for indexing purposes, specifying which file the string belongs to and at what point in the file it is located, so allowing a single file to be made up of many strings.

To avoid errors that occur during both writing and reading, a particular problem when neighboring bases are of the same variety, data is encoded in trits – digits with the values 0, 1 or 2 – and stipulate that a given trit is represented by one of the three bases not used to code the trit immediately preceding it. An additional measure was to copy the final 75% of each string into the start of the successive string.

The team tested the scheme by encoding five data files into single DNA sequences and then split those sequences up into roughly 150,000 individual strings, all 117 bases long. Fittingly, one of the files was a PDF of Watson and Crick's famous double-helix paper – successfully encoded into double helices.

The text of Shakespeare's sonnets and an audio recording of Martin Luther King's "I have a dream" speech were also stored in MP3 format. The team then uploaded the encoded files to a private webpage to enable Agilent Technologies in California to synthesize the DNA. This involved using a sophisticated kind of inkjet printer to fire chemical reagents onto a microscope slide in such a way as to add one molecule at a time to a growing string of DNA, and then repeating the process to produce the thousands of strings required.

Sent as a tiny quantity of powder at room temperature and without specialized packaging, the DNA arrived in Heidelberg, Germany, at the main site of the European Molecular Biology Laboratory, of which the European Bioinformatics Institute is a part. After being put into solution the DNA was read, or "sequenced", using a now fairly standard laboratory machine, and the resulting series of bases was then decoded on a computer to reproduce the five files. Four of the files were identical copies of the originals, while the fifth required some minor adjustment to recover its full set of data.

Goldman and colleagues claim to have achieved a density of 2 petabytes (10^{15} bytes) per gram of DNA which, they calculate, would allow at least 100 million hours of high-definition video to be stored in a teacup. Their DNA sample was therefore very small. "In our test tube the DNA looks like a speck of dust," says Goldman. "In fact the sample is so small that when it arrived it looked like the test tube was empty."

Unlike tapes, which need to be periodically rewritten, DNA remains unchanged as long as it is stored somewhere that is cold, dry and dark.

The latest research is published in *Nature*.

Another article can be found in the on line magazine, "Extreme Tech" 2/20/2012, which quotes the magazine Karlsruhe Institue of Technology (1/16/2012):

In order to find a method for more cost-effective data storage, a group of researchers from the DFG-Center for Functional Nanostructures (CFN) at the Karlsruhe Institute of Technology (KIT) in Germany and the National Tsing Hua University in Taiwan have created a DNA-based "write-once-read-many-times" (WORM) memory device.

The device consists of a thin film of salmon DNA, which has been embedded with nano-sized particles of silver and then sandwiched between two electrodes. Ultraviolet light is used to encode information. The concept is published in Applied Physics Letter.

The collaboration on these devices started more than a year ago, and was a productive cross-field/cross-country endeavor. Dr. Ljiljana Fruk heads an interdisciplinary research group at the CFN concerned with DNA nanotechnology, biofunctionalization and light triggered nanodevice design and was involved in the development of the light triggered, DNA templated nanoparticle production and its characterization. Dr. Yu-Chueh Hung's group on the other side used this knowledge to optimize the process and design the functional memory device. The transmission electron microscope (TEM) images of the nanoparticles in the DNA were obtained in turn by the Nanostructure Service Laboratory in the CFN.

As described in the article, shining UV light on the system causes the silver atoms to cluster into nano-sized particles. These particles provide the platform for the data encoding. The device is able to hold charge under a low current, which corresponds to the off-state. Under a high electrical field the charges pass through the device, which then corresponds to the on-state.

The team in Taiwan found that once the system had been turned on, it stayed on; changing the voltage across the electrodes did not change the system's conductivity. This means that information can be written to the device but not overwritten. Once written, the device appears to retain that information indefinitely. The researchers report that the material's conductivity did not change significantly during nearly 30 hours of tracking.

The authors expect the technique to be useful in the design of optical storage devices and suggest that it may have plasmonic applications as well. This work combines new advances in DNA nanotechnology with conventional polymer fabrication platform to realize novel DNA-based organic devices. It demonstrates new possibilities to fabricate novel, cheaper and bio friendly devices by integrating and merging several fields of interest.

Are we designed and pre-written memory devices? Do we carry

within our DNA knowledge of an ancient civilization, their history, technology, and culture? Are the various species inhabiting the planet earth chapters in this book? Are we pre-programmed to evolve as this history is being written within our very cells?

Is our physical evolution being guided? Our spiritual evolution tends to bare out the change in the interactions between these gods and mankind. Does our mental evolution likewise reflect their influence?

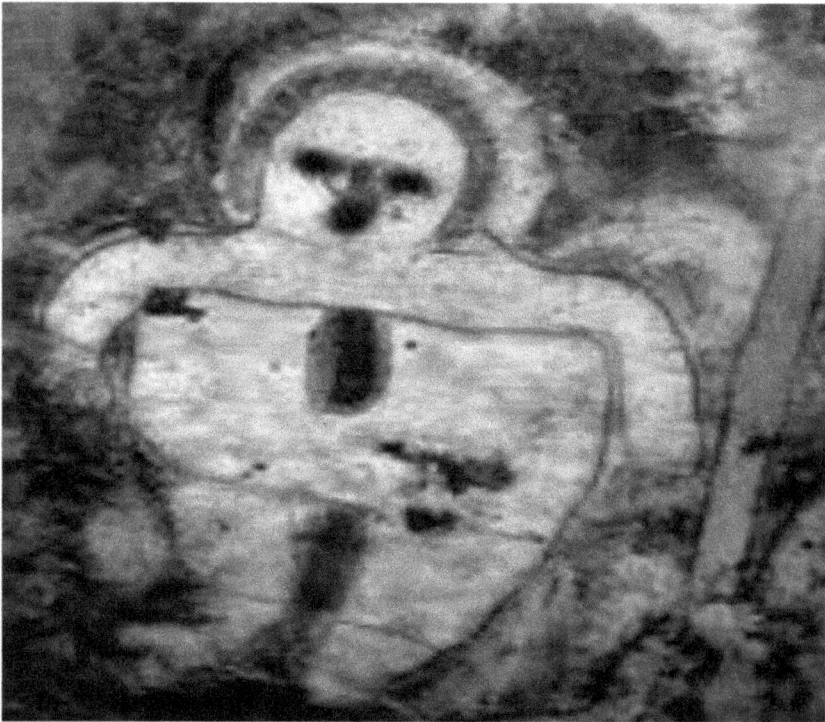

Pictures from Kimberley, Australia dated to 5,000 BC

Ninety-five percent of our DNA is NOT involved in the formation and reproduction of humans. Scientist call this "junk" DNA. It is not junk DNA. It is encoded data. Ninety-five percent of our DNA is being used to store alien data, history, and technology. Five percent is simply overhead to replicate and maintain the data in the form of the human carrier, but what an elegant carrier it is, designed to conquer environments and survive until needed.

The God Program

The concept of god seems to appear around the same time humans began to express themselves through arts and crafts. This makes sense because there would be no way for modern man to know what our forefathers were thinking except via writing or art. Their expanded ability to express themselves reveals to us their ideas of god.

Through the ages, humans have believed in a god, or gods, but what drove mankind to create or express the idea of god? Whether sun, moon, or idols of wood or stone, humans all over the world invented or expressed their own ideas of god. When presented with the vision of an advanced society with such a simple device as a flashlight, the idea of the sun god is born. Man depicted gods based on what powers they witnessed at the time. These powers were likely basic technologies of an advanced people.

As one leader, El, divided mankind into separate parcels, mankind went from monotheism to polytheism. This is the story of those changing views of god, which took us from monotheism to polytheism and idolatry back to what one might view as a "modified" monotheism.

We should take a deep breath and examine modern religions. We would find many are modified monotheism. We may have one God, but most Christians believe there is a trinity, meaning there are three gods in one. In many religions there are angels, as well as an antagonist such as Satan. These are powerful beings made to do God's bidding. Not all religions agree with the placement of angels or Satan.

"We despise all reverences and all objects of reverence which are outside the pale of our list of sacred things and yet, with strange inconsistency, we are shocked when other people despise and defile the things which are holy for us" - Mark Twain

In the recesses of time, when humankind began to search for and conceive of "god", the idea of a single, powerful, father figure was born. This "god" was a reflection of the life they led in a patriarchal society with a head of a family or tribe guiding them. Possibly, monotheism is the oldest and most enduring form of religion. This is impossible to prove, however, there is some evidence coming from ancient, untouched tribes that shows a very old and unbroken religious lineage of worshipping a single god above all others.

Primitive cultures did not worship the same god or recognize tribal gods as the same deity. They acknowledged the existence of other gods of neighboring tribes, but chose to worship their own idea of the creator or high god. Their form of worship included the sacrifice of animals and humans, with an eye toward appeasing or influencing their god. They worshipped through rites, rituals, and ceremonies led by priests and holy men whom they believed to be intuitively connected with their deity. How can one believe in other gods and still be monotheistic? It comes down to a focus of worship.

Outside the Bible, the oldest records of religion come from Ebla in Syria. The ancient city of Ebla once was situated where Tell Mardikh is today, about half way between Hamath and Aleppo. There is a mound and a small village about one kilometer off the highway where excavations began in the 1960's. In the 1970's, a series of tablets were discovered among the ruins.

These 17,000 tablets became known as "The Ebla Tablets." They were originally discovered under the direction of two professors from the University of Rome, Dr. Paolo Matthiae and Dr. Giovanni Petinato. These tablets appear to have been written during the last two generations of ancient Ebla, around 2300 to 2250 B.C. Even more extraordinary was the discovery of "a creation hymn" in the tablets. Three different versions of the Eblaite "creation hymn" were found. Dr. Petinato translated one of the creation hymns as follows:

"Lord of heaven and earth: the earth was not, you created it, the light of day was not, you created it, the morning light you had not [yet] made exist."

These tablets, written long ago, are established proof of monotheism. Here is strong evidence of early monotheism that refutes the theory that monotheism was born from some consolidation or evolution of polytheism. Additionally, the fact that systems and ideas tend to begin in simplicity and end in complexity backs up this evidence. This could possibly follow the pattern of society. In fact, the idea of polytheism could have evolved along side the beginning of the specialization of gods within the human community. Polytheism could have begun when tribes with certain gods interfaced with other tribes with different gods, each taking and worshipping the additional god as a lesser deity.

Ancient Ebla was primarily a pagan culture having gods such as Dagon, Baal, and Ishtar that were very important to the people of that time. Conversely, they conceived of one true and powerful God, with the lesser gods serving as his sons and servants. These sons and servants are the forerunners of the angels and demons of today's religions.

The theory that monotheism was the earliest form of worship is further bolstered as we look to Africa, the continent that scientists believe is the birthplace of humankind. The traceable, primitive religions of Africa all reveal an explicit monotheism. The noted authority on African religions, John S. Mbiti, wrote about the 300 traditional religions in Africa. He states, "In all these societies, without a single exception, people believed in a god, who was the

Supreme Being." Their belief in a sky-god bears this out.

In 1912, Father Wilhelm Schmidt wrote extensively about the idea of primitive monotheism in his book, "The Origin of the Idea of God." In the book he asked a question. Was the idea of a remote god who was absent in the daily life of his subjects, impossible for the primitives to continually relate to? Was it the absence of frequent interaction or was it the abrupt change from a single god to a cadre' of ruling deities overseeing us that was the root of polytheism?

Religions begin with simple revelations or beliefs and become more ritual, ceremony, and doctrine ridden over time. God is lost within the maze of diverging beliefs. This was and is the case with religion in general. Myths and a multitude of stories developed to prove the power of these various gods as one tribe began to claim their god was better.

What purpose did the religions of the ancients serve? As they constructed and developed their myths, were they telling stories of an ancient god who came down from the sky? As mankind turned from monotheism to polytheism were we influenced in this because El gave his various lieutenants control over us, each with their own ways, desires, and personalities?

As we saw and interacted with these beings less and less did we simply revert back to monotheism because it was programmed in us to do so? If one wishes to keep a species in control why not program in an innate reverence?

Nowhere has that idea received a more intriguing going-over than in the recently published book, "The God Gene: How Faith Is Hardwired into Our Genes" (Doubleday; 256 pages), by molecular biologist Dean Hamer. Chief of gene structure at the National Cancer Institute, Hamer not only claims that human spirituality is an adaptive trait, but he also says he has located one of the genes responsible, a gene that just happens to also code for production of the neurotransmitters that regulate our moods. Our most profound feelings of spirituality, according to a literal reading of Hamer's work, may be due to little more than an occasional shot of intoxicating brain chemicals governed by our DNA. "I'm a believer that every thought we think and every feeling we feel is the result of activity in the brain," Hamer says. "I think we follow the basic law of nature, which is that we're a bunch of chemical reactions running around in a bag."

"Hamer began looking in 1998, when he was conducting a survey on smoking and addiction for the National Cancer Institute. As part of his study, he recruited more than 1,000 men and women, who agreed to take a standardized, 240-question personality test called the Temperament and Character Inventory (TCI). Among the traits the TCI measures is one known as self-transcendence, which consists of three other traits: self-forgetfulness, or the ability to get entirely lost in an experience; transpersonal identification, or a feeling of connectedness to a larger universe; and mysticism, or an openness to things not literally provable. Put them all together, and you come as close as science can to measuring what it feels like to be spiritual. "This allows us to have the kind of experience described as religious ecstasy," says Robert Cloninger, a psychiatrist at Washington University in St. Louis, Mo., and the designer of the self-transcendence portion of the TCI."

"Hamer decided to use the data he gathered in the smoking survey to conduct a little spirituality study on the side. First he ranked the participants along Cloninger's self-transcendence scale, placing them on a continuum from least to most spiritually inclined. Then he went poking around in their genes to see if he could find the DNA responsible for the differences. Spelunking in the human genome is not easy, what with 35,000 genes consisting of 3.2 billion chemical bases. To narrow the field, Hamer confined his work to nine specific genes known to play major roles in the production of monoamines--brain chemicals, including serotonin, norepinephrine and dopamine, that regulate such fundamental functions as mood and motor control. Some of these chemicals are known to be used in religious rituals.

Studying the nine candidate genes in DNA samples provided by his subjects, Hamer quickly hit the genetic jackpot. A variation in a gene known as VMAT2--for vesicular monoamine transporter-- seemed to be directly related to how the volunteers scored on the self-transcendence test. "

"At least one faith, according to one of its best-known scholars, formalizes the idea of gene-based spirituality and even puts a pretty spin on it. Buddhists, says Robert Thurman, professor of Buddhist studies at Columbia University, have long entertained the idea that we inherit a spirituality gene from the person we were in a previous life. Smaller than an ordinary gene, it combines with two larger physical genes we inherit from our parents, and together they shape our physical and spiritual profile. Says Thurman: "The spiritual gene helps establish a general trust in the universe, a sense of openness and generosity."

"Other researchers have taken the science in a different direction, looking not for the genes that code for spirituality but for how that spirituality plays out in the brain. Neuroscientist Andrew Newberg of the University of Pennsylvania School of Medicine has used several types of imaging systems to watch the brains of subjects as they meditate or pray. By measuring blood flow, he determines which regions are responsible for the feelings the volunteers experience. The deeper that people descend into meditation or prayer, Newberg found, the more active the frontal lobe and the limbic system become. The frontal lobe is the seat of concentration and attention; the limbic system is where powerful feelings, including rapture, are processed. More revealing is the fact that at the same time these regions flash to life, another important region--the parietal lobe at the back of the brain--goes dim. It's this lobe that orients the individual in time and space."

"Of course, concepts of God reside in the brain. They certainly don't reside in the toe," says Lindon Eaves, director of the Virginia Institute for Psychiatric and Behavioral Genetics at Virginia Commonwealth University in Richmond. "The question is, To what is this wiring responsive? Why is it there?" Says Paul Davies, professor of natural philosophy at Macquarie University in Sydney, Australia: "I think a lot of people make the mistake of thinking that if you explain something, you explain it away. I don't see that at all with religious experience."

"Those religious believers who are comfortable with the idea that God genes are the work of God should have little trouble making the next leap: that not only are the genes there but they are central to our survival, one of the hinges upon which the very evolution of the human species turned. It's an argument that's not terribly hard to make."

"One of the best examples of religion as social organizer, according to Binghamton University's Wilson, is early Calvinism. John Calvin rose to prominence in 1536 when, as a theologian and religious reformer, he was recruited to help bring order to the fractious city of Geneva. Calvin, perhaps one of the greatest theological minds ever produced by European Christianity, was a lawyer by trade. Wilson speculates that it was Calvin's pragmatic genius to understand that while civil laws alone might not be enough to bring the city's deadbeats and other malefactors into line, divine law might be."

"Nonetheless, sticking points do remain that prevent genetic theory from going down smoothly. One that's particularly troublesome is the question of why Hamer's God-gene, or any of the others that may eventually be discovered--is distributed so unevenly among us. Why are some of us spiritual virtuosos, while others can't play a note? Isn't it one of the central tenets of religion that grace is available to everybody? At least a few scientists shrug at the question. "Some get religion, and some don't," says Virginia Commonwealth University's Eaves..." --*With reporting by Jeff Chu/ London, Broward Liston/ Orlando, Maggie Sieger/ Chicago and Daniel Williams/ Sydney*

Some get religion and some don't. The gene is distributed unequally within the population. Scientists do not know why. Is this the "boundary" spoken of in the scriptures? Is this the tool of predestination? Is this God's mark for heaven or hell? We would believe we have free will and the gene would give that impression. Yet, from our birth, and maybe from the very thought of us by God in the beginning of time, we were predestined because of the "The God Gene."

We can answer the question of the unevenly distributed God-gene. The God-gene was introduced into humans to ensure our worship and slavery to the gods of old. With the introduction of alien DNA from the angelic interbreeding with women the puzzle is solved. The DNA of the Watchers would have no such gene, only the women would have carried the God-gene. This also answers the question as to why the women went along with the procreation so willingly. They were marrying their gods, whom they reverenced deeply. They were designed to do so. However, the hybrids that came from the union would be mutants. The God-gene would be compromised, suppressed, or destroyed in some of the offspring. Other interesting mutations occurred. Intellect and strength increased and in some, such as the heroes of old and certain abilities manifested, which were so superior to men they would be called gods and sons of god. Did the Watchers save us from slavery intentionally or was it a byproduct of their desire to experience human love?

Genetic lines occasionally produced men of peace and power, with amazing compassion and healing powers. Other times the recessive traits would not be so kind. Generally, mankind grew in intellect and reason as we evolved toward our makers and like them we began to reach for the stars.

Indian Vimana

Timeline: Putting the Pieces Together

In the beginning the gods created the heavens and the earth. These advanced beings, aliens, or God's, created mankind. They did so one strand of DNA at a time. Bit by bit, byte by byte, block by block, they built the human genome. Thus were created Adam and Eve, beings of pure programmed DNA. Hidden within the programmed DNA was a single gene called "the God Gene", which ensured reverence and obedience to our makers.

At this juncture of the hypothesis it must be stated clearly that if our race was spawned by a more advanced race it in no way negates the existence of a real deity. If we were created by another race one must, for the sake of logic, ask who or what created them, and so on, back into time until one comes to some prime causality or first maker from which all things began. At that point one may discover beings gifted with dimensional or temporal travel placing them beyond our comprehension. Or, one may simply find we are staring into the face of the almighty.

As mankind began to multiply upon the face of the earth these beings or gods fell in love with their own creation. The aliens who were sent to monitor mankind, called the watchers, came down and took women and had intercourse with them. Two-hundred watchers abandoned their post and their assignment to monitor, observe, and report on the deeds and conditions of the humans they had developed.

By injecting alien DNA in the human genome, anomalies began to occur. Offspring of the matings between Angels and women produced Giants, men of renown, and monsters. The experiment had been compromised and the DNA so carefully produced was contaminated. The effect of the god gene was reduced in some and destroyed in others. Intellect was increased, but so were mutations.

To save the experiment all humans on earth with the exception of eight humans were exterminated. Four of the male humans came from a single bloodline and four female humans came from separate bloodlines. With these limited variances within the DNA it was hoped that the contamination could be kept to a minimum and the experiment could go on.

Even though the DNA contamination had spread to all of the bloodlines, it could be monitored and adjusted.

The purity of the DNA within the human genome was important to the aliens or gods because encoded in it was the sum total of the history, knowledge, and records of their dying society. With the development of mankind the gods were able to pass along their humanness and their knowledge. The wisdom and technology of their race would not be lost. In time if any survived they would be able to come back and by extracting a few cells harvest all knowledge of their ancient past.

Those who made us may not be the one from whom all things began. Our makers may be advanced beings, much like ourselves, who were seeking to do on a grander scale those things we have just become capable of doing. We are creating DNA, manipulating genes, and creating new forms of life. We manipulate gene lines in our plants and call them hybrid corn and wheat. We manipulate bloodlines in our dogs and cats and call them new breeds. So the aliens or gods watch over and control our genetic path, as well as the genetic path of plants and animals on earth. They did not want man accidentally changing what they had done.

Hybridization by humans is against the law laid down in the Bible

Leviticus 19:19 New International Version (NIV)
19 "'Keep my decrees.
"'Do not mate different kinds of animals.
"'Do not plant your field with two kinds of seed.
"'Do not wear clothing woven of two kinds of material.

Deuteronomy 22:9 New International Version (NIV)
9 Do not plant two kinds of seed in your vineyard; if you do, not only the crops you plant but also the fruit of the vineyard will be defiled

As the remaining bloodline on earth began to grow in the human population began to expand once again the commander or high God decided to break the earth and its inhabitants into parcels to be overseen by his lieutenants. Thus, in the time of the most ancient humans, monotheism was the only accepted practice but in the time that humans were given to other lesser gods the idea of polytheism was born and each country or section of the country related to its own God.

The most ancient texts and oldest Scriptures bear this out, that in the beginning it was El and his counsel creating and overseeing the human race. But when his creation was spoiled those who vandalized it were exiled and those who took women as wives were left on earth. Here they stayed and taught us. We learned from the arts of herbology, metalworking, alchemy which came to be known as chemistry, astronomy which came to be known as astrology, biogenetics, and warfare. We also learned architecture, geometry, math, and the power of the mind, which came to be known as spells or charms.

As the experiment was brought into tolerance and those who were left behind vanished, died, or were recaptured and placed in prison for treason, there was less and less reason for the interaction between gods and humans. All that was needed from that point was occasional random samplings of DNA from various humans to ensure that the experiment was still within tolerance and being carried on, as it should.

Of course, there is another, equally intriguing scenario. What if the watchers rebelled against their commanders because they wished to save the human race from slavery and experimentation?

Seeing the potential in the human race and knowing we were in our evolution as they once were eons ago, the watchers may have attempted to save mankind. This would explain why they stayed with us and taught us all of the arts and sciences listed in the old texts. It would explain the statement made by El to the Watchers: "I know you love your children, but you will watch them all die." The mutants and giants coming from intercourse could have been unforeseen consequences, but they loved these children nonetheless.

Did the Watchers stay and teach us because they were stranded, or did they stay out of a sense of duty and love? Either way, they could not save us from the alterations already done to our genetic code.

Still having the God Gene within its DNA structure mankind is pulled toward worship of a higher being. With polytheism no longer supported by the appearance of various Angels or gods in the time of visitation and monitoring past, mankind began to once again adopt monotheism.

In every culture and in most religions mankind awaits the reunion with their God. We are programmed for the best possible outcome should our creators come back to correct our course genetically, harvest their programming, or cohabitate with us once again.

It is now a waiting game, a game of hide-and-go-seek millions of years in the playing. God is with us and in us no less than a creature reflects the personality and thoughts of it creator.. We can see our Creator in us but we are programmed to yearn for his touch so that we may complete our task. If we knew the language, if we knew the algorithm, if we knew the code, we could decipher what the human genome really means in its digital format. We have discovered and mapped the human genome. All we need is the Rosetta Stone for the translation. Sitting within us is a complete Encyclopedia of alien history and knowledge. The book is closed and all we need do is open it and read.

We have all knowledge within us – all we need do is to know ourselves.

About the Ancient Texts

Various ancient Jewish and Christian texts were referenced in this book. All of them can be found at www.fifthestatepub.com.

The Dead Sea Scrolls found in the caves of Qumran are of great interest in the task of clarifying the history and doctrine in existence between biblical times and the fixing of canon. The scrolls were penned in the second century B.C. and were in use at least until the destruction of the second temple in 70 A.D. Similar scrolls to those found in the eleven caves of Qumran were also found at the Masada stronghold which fell to the Romans in 73 A.D.

Fragments of every book of the Old Testament except Esther were found in the caves of Qumran, as were many other ancient books. Some of these books are considered to have been of equal importance and influence to the people of Qumran and to the writers and scholars of the time. Writers of the New Testament were among those studying the scrolls found in Qumran. Knowing this, one might ask which of the dozens of non-canonical books most influenced the writers of the New Testament.

It is possible to ascertain the existence of certain influences within the Bible context by using the Bible itself. The Bible can direct us to other works in three ways. The work can be mentioned by name, as is the Book of Jasher. The work can be quoted within the Bible text, as is the case with the Book of Enoch. The existence of the work can be alluded to, as is the case of the missing letter from the apostle Paul to the Corinthians.

In the case of those books named in the Bible, one can compile a list. The list is lengthier than one might suspect. Most of these works have not been found. Some have been unearthed but their authenticity is questioned. Others have been recovered and the link between scripture and scroll is generally accepted.

The Book of Jasher

Jasher is not the author's name. Rather, it carries the meaning of something straight, true, or upright. The meaning could be the upright book or the faithful record, or it could refer to the character and reliability of the person(s) making the record.

The Bible references The Book of Jasher as a source of information and history in at least two places.

In the Book of Joshua is the account of an event that staggers the mind.

"And the sun stood still, and the moon stayed, until the people had avenged themselves upon their enemies. Is not this written in the book of Jasher? So the sun stood still in the midst of heaven, and hasted not to go down about a whole day." Joshua 10:13

One translation of a parallel chapter in the Book of Jasher states as follows:

"And when they were smiting, the day was declining toward evening, and Joshua said in the sight of all the people, Sun, stand thou still upon Gibeon, and thou moon in the valley of Ajalon, until the nation shall have revenged itself upon its enemies. And the Lord hearkened to the voice of Joshua, and the sun stood still in the midst of the heavens, and it stood still six and thirty moments, and the moon also stood still and hastened not to go down a whole day." Jasher 88:63-64

Another Biblical reference to Jasher shows David teaching archery to his army:

"Also he bade them teach the children of Judah the use of the bow; behold, it is written in the book of Jasher." 2 Samuel 1:18

The Jews of the first century A.D. held the Book of Jasher as a reliable historical document, although not "inspired." When Titus destroyed Jerusalem in A.D. 70, one of his officers discovered a hidden library complete with a scholar hiding there. The officer had mercy on the man and took him and the books to his residence at Seville, Spain, (which was at that time the capital of the Roman province Hispalensis). The manuscript was later donated to the Jewish college at Cordova, Spain; and after printing was invented, the Jewish scholars had the book printed in Hebrew in Venice in 1625.

Confusion arose when another book of the same title was translated and released. This book, known now as Pseudo-Jasher, was discovered to be a hoax. Scholars turned against that book but continued to confuse it with the older document of the same name.

One of the printed manuscripts of Jasher from Spain was acquired by a British citizen named Samuel. Samuel set about to translate the book into English. When the British scholars heard of this, they made no distinction between the two books of Jasher and Pseudo-Jasher and the climate for publication turned stormy. Samuel sold his translation to Mordecai M. Noah, a New York publisher, who published it in 1840 as the first English translation.

The copyright was later obtained by J. H. Parry and Company of Salt Lake City, Utah in 1887. It is a modern rendition of this version presented here.

The book seems to contain authentic Hebrew traditions and phraseology. Jasher, being a record, was added to and updated by each Hebrew historian as the book was handed down.

The book of Jasher we possess today was likely composed by an author compiling many old Jewish traditions (called Midrash) dating back to around the time of Christ. This included the source from the rescue of 70 A.D. Scholars agree that the Book of Jasher was likely last updated in Spain about the twelfth century A.D. It is difficult to know if Jasher is quoting Midrash literature, or if Midrash literature was quoting the real Book of Jasher, which was also quoted in the Old Testament.

"Midrash" refers to writings containing extra-legal material of anecdotal or allegorical nature, designed either to clarify historical material, or to teach a moral point.

The names of the countries in which the sons of Noah are reported to have settled can definitely be dated to the eleventh century in Spain. This does not make it conclusive that the entire work must have been authored at that time. As books are copied, scribes can take it upon themselves to place the current names in the text.

Although Jasher was not considered inspired, it was considered to be a historical record reliable enough to be quoted by prophets and kings.

There are differences in authority and weight given to various types of records. Civil and historical records may serve the same historical purpose or record, but texts thought to be inspired have both historical and spiritual function.

When Ptolemy, King of Egypt, requested the Jewish holy books, the Israelites felt they could not give the Gentiles their sacred texts, so they sent him the Book of Jasher. He cherished it but later found it had a lesser status than the scriptures. Angry about the hoax, he confronted the Jews. Now with their heads at risk, they agreed to translate their Old Testament into Greek, which became known as the Septuagint.

The Lost Book of Enoch

Of all the books quoted, paraphrased, or referred to in the Bible, the Book of Enoch has influenced the writers of the Bible as few others have. The writers of the New Testament were frequently influenced by other writings, which set the theology and beliefs of the day. One of the main sources of theology regarding angels, demons, and the watchers was the Book of Enoch.

If a book is mentioned or quoted in the Bible is it not worthy of further study? The Book of Enoch was once cherished by Jews and Christians alike. It is still read today in certain Coptic Christian Churches in Ethiopia and is considered equal to all other books of the Bible.

Two versions of the Book of Enoch exist today. Most scholars date the Book of Enoch to sometime during the second century B.C. We do not know what earlier oral tradition, if any, the book contains. Enoch was considered inspired and authentic by certain Jewish sects of the first century B.C. and remained popular for at least five hundred years. The earliest Ethiopian text was apparently derived from a Greek manuscript of the Book of Enoch, which itself was a copy of an earlier text. The original was apparently written in the Semitic language, now thought to be Aramaic.

The Book of Enoch was discovered in the 18th century. It was thought that Enoch was penned after beginning of the Christian era. This theory was based upon the fact that it had quotes and paraphrases as well as concepts found in the New Testament. Thus, it was assumed that Enoch was heavily influenced by writers such as Jude and Peter.

However, recent discoveries of copies of the book among the Dead Sea Scrolls prove the book existed long before the time of Jesus Christ. These scrolls force a closer look and reconsideration. It becomes obvious that the New Testament did not influence the Book of Enoch; on the contrary, the Book of Enoch influenced the New Testament.

The date of the original writing upon which the second century B.C. Qumran copies were based is shrouded in obscurity. Likewise lost are the sources of the oral traditions that came to be the Book of Enoch.

It has been largely the opinion of historians that the book

does not really contain the authentic words of the ancient prophet named Enoch, since he would have lived several thousand years earlier than the first known appearance of the book attributed to him. However, the first century Christians accepted the Book of Enoch as inspired, if not authentic.

They relied on it to understand the origin and purpose of many things, from angels to wind, sun, and stars. In fact, many of the key concepts used by Jesus Christ himself seem directly connected to terms and ideas in the Book of Enoch.

It is hard to avoid the evidence that Jesus not only studied the book, but also respected it highly enough to allude to its doctrine and content. Enoch is replete with mentions of the coming kingdom and other holy themes. It was not only Jesus who quoted phases or ideas from Enoch, there are over one hundred comments in the New Testament which find precedence in the Book of Enoch.

Other evidence of the early Christians' acceptance of the Book of Enoch was for many years buried under the King James Bible's mistranslation of Luke 9:35, describing the transfiguration of Christ: "And there came a voice out of the cloud, saying, 'This is my beloved Son. Hear him.'" Apparently, the translator wished to make this verse agree with a similar verse in Matthew and Mark. But Luke's verse in the original Greek reads: "This is my Son, the Elect One (from the Greek ho eklelegmenos, "the elect one"). Hear him."

The "Elect One" is a most significant term (found fourteen times) in the Book of Enoch. If the book was indeed known to the apostles of Christ, with its abundant descriptions of the Elect One who should "sit upon the throne of glory" and the Elect One who should "dwell in the midst of them," then the great scriptural authenticity is justly accorded to the Book of Enoch when the "voice out of the cloud" tells the apostles, "This is my Son, the Elect One." The one promised in the Book of Enoch.

The Book of Jude tells us in verse 14 that "Enoch, the seventh from Adam, prophesied." Jude, in verse 15, makes a direct reference to the Book of Enoch, where he writes, "to execute judgment on all, to convict all who are ungodly." As a matter of fact, it is a direct, word-for-word quote. Therefore, Jude's reference to the Enochian prophesies strongly leans toward the conclusion that these written prophecies were available to him at that time.

Fragments of ten Enoch manuscripts were found among the Dead Sea Scrolls. The number of scrolls indicates the Essenes (a Jewish commune or sect at the time of Christ) could well have used the Enochian writings as a community prayer book or teacher's manual and study text.

Many of the early church fathers also supported the Enochian writings. Justin Martyr ascribed all evil to demons he alleged to be the offspring of the angels who fell through lust for women; directly referencing the Enochian writings.

Athenagoras (170 A.D.) regarded Enoch as a true prophet. He describes the angels who "violated both their own nature and their office." In his writings, he goes into detail about the nature of fallen angels and the cause of their fall, which comes directly from the Enochian writings.

Since any book stands to be interpreted in many ways, Enoch posed problems for some theologians. Instead of reexamining their own theology, they sought to dispose of that which went counter to their beliefs. Some of the visions in Enoch are believed to point to the consummation of the age in conjunction with Christ's second coming which some believe took place in A.D. 70 (in the destruction of Jerusalem).

This being the case, it should not surprise us that Enoch was declared a fake and was rejected by Hilary, Jerome, and Augustine. Enoch was subsequently lost to Western Christendom for over a thousand years.

Enoch's "seventy generations" was also a great problem. Many scholars thought it could not be made to stretch beyond the First Century. Copies of Enoch soon disappeared. Indeed, for almost two thousand years we knew only the references made to it in the Bible. Without having the book itself, we could not have known it was being quoted in the Bible, sometimes word for word by Peter and Jude.

"...the Lord, having saved a people out of the land of Egypt, afterward destroyed them that believed not. And angels that kept not their own principality, but left their proper habitation, he hath kept in everlasting bonds under darkness unto the judgment of the great day. Even as Sodom and Gomorrah, and the cities about them...in like manner...are set out as examples...." Jude 5-7

"For if God spared not the angels when they sinned, but cast them down into hell, and committed them to pits of darkness, to be reserved unto judgment," 2 Peter 2-4.

To what extent other New Testament writers regarded Enoch as scriptural canon may be determined by comparing their writings with those found in Enoch. A strong possibility of influence upon their thought and choice of wording is evidenced by a great many references found in Enoch which remind one of passages found in the New Testament.

The Book of Enoch seems to be a missing link between Jewish and Christian theology and is considered by many to be more Christian in its theology than Jewish. It was considered scripture by many early Christians. The literature of the church fathers is filled with references to this book. The early second century apocryphal book of the Epistle of Barnabas makes many references and quotes from the Book of Enoch. Second and third century church fathers like Justin Martyr, Irenaeus, Origin and Clement of Alexandria all seemed to have accepted Enoch as authentic. Tertullian (160-230 A.D.) even called the Book of Enoch, "Holy Scripture."

The Ethiopian Coptic Church holds the Book of Enoch as part of its official spiritual canon. It was widely known and read the first three centuries after Christ. This and many other books became discredited after the Council of Laodicea. And being under ban of the authorities, it gradually disappeared from circulation.

In 1773, rumors of a surviving copy of the book drew Scottish explorer James Bruce to distant Ethiopia. He found the Book of Enoch had been preserved by the Ethiopian church, which put it right alongside the other books of the Bible.

Bruce secured not one, but three Ethiopian copies of the book and brought them back to Europe and Britain. In 1773 Bruce returned from six years in Abyssinia. In 1821 Richard Laurence published the first English translation. The famous R.H. Charles edition was published in 1912. In the following years several portions of the Greek text surfaced. Then with the discovery of cave 4 at Qumran, seven fragmentary copies of the Aramaic text were discovered.

Even in its complete form, the Book of Enoch is not one manuscript. It is a composite of several manuscripts written by several authors. Enoch and Noah each have pieces of the book ascribed to them. Yet still today the most complete text of the multifaceted book is the Ethiopian copy.

Later, another "Book of Enoch" surfaced. This text, dubbed "2 Enoch" and commonly called "the Slavonic Enoch," was discovered in 1886 by Professor Sokolov in the archives of the Belgrade Public Library. It appears that just as the Ethiopian Enoch ("1 Enoch") escaped the sixth-century Church suppression of Enoch texts in the Mediterranean area, so a Slavonic Enoch survived far away, long after the originals from which it was copied were destroyed or hidden.

Specialists in the Enochian texts believe that the missing original from which the Slavonic was copied was probably a Greek manuscript, which itself may have been based on a Hebrew or Aramaic manuscript.

The Slavonic text is evidence of many later additions to the original manuscript. Unfortunately, later additions and the deletion of teachings considered erroneous, rendered the text unreliable.

Because of certain references to dates and data regarding certain calendar systems in the Slavonic Enoch, some claim the text cannot be earlier than the seventh century A.D. Some see these passages not as evidence of Christian authorship, but as later Christian interpolations into an earlier manuscript. Enochian specialist R.H. Charles, for instance, believes that even the better of the two Slavonic manuscripts contains interpolations and is, in textual terms, "corrupt." It is for the reasons above, we will look only at the book referred to as 1 Enoch. We will leave the inferior manuscript of 2 Enoch for another day.

The translations used for this work are taken from both the Richard Laurence and R.H. Charles manuscripts in addition to numerous sources and commentaries. The texts were compared and, in some cases, transliterated for easier reading by the modern "American" English reader as some phrasing from the 18th and 19th centuries may seem somewhat clumsy to our 21st century eyes.

The Second Book of Enoch: Slavonic Enoch

As part of the Enochian literature, The Second Book of Enoch is included in the pseudepigraphal corpus.

Pseudepigrapha : Spurious or pseudonymous writings, especially Jewish writings ascribed to various biblical patriarchs and prophets but composed within approximately 200 years of the birth of Jesus Christ.

In 1773, rumors of a surviving copy of an ancient book drew Scottish explorer James Bruce to distant Ethiopia. There, he found the "First Book of Enoch." Later, another "Book of Enoch" surfaced. The text, which is known as "Second Enoch," was discovered in 1886 by Professor Sokolov in the archives of the Belgrade Public Library. The Second Book of Enoch was written in the latter half of the first century A.D. The text was preserved only in Slavonic and consequently bears the designation, "Slavonic Enoch." The text has also been known by the titles of "2 Enoch", and "The Secrets of Enoch." 2 Enoch is basically an expansion of Genesis 5:21-32, taking the reader from the time of Enoch to the onset of the great flood of Noah's day.

The main theme of the book is the ascension of Enoch progressively through multiple heavens. During the ascension Enoch is transfigured into an angel and granted access to the secrets of creation. Enoch is then given a 30 day grace period to return to earth and instruct his sons and all the members of his household regarding everything God had revealed to him. The text reports that after period of grace an angel will then come to retrieve him to take him from the earth.

Many credible versions end with chapter 68, however there is a longer version of 2 Enoch, which we will examine. In this version the wisdom and insights given to the family of Enoch is passed from family members to Melchizedek, whom God raises up as an archpriest. Melchizedek then fulfills the function of a prophet-priest. To pave the way to Melchizedek, Methuselah functions as a priest for ten years and then passed his station on to Nir, Noah's younger brother. Nir's wife, Sopanim, miraculously conceives without human intercourse while about to die and posthumously gives birth to Melchizedek, who is born with the appearance and maturity of a three-year old child and the symbol of the priesthood on his chest.

The world is doomed to suffer the flood but Michael the archangel promises Melchizedek salvation. This establishes his priesthood for all of eternity. The text goes on to report that in the last generation, there will be another Melchizedek who will be "the head of all, a great archpriest, the Word and

Power of God, who will perform miracles, greater and more glorious than all the previous ones".

The manuscripts, which contain and preserve this document, exist only in Old Slavonic. Of the twenty or more manuscripts dating from the 13th century A.D. no single one contains the complete text of 2 Enoch. When pieced together there appears to be two versions. These we will refer to as the long and short version.

The difference in length between the two is due to two quite different features. There are blocks of text found only in the longer manuscripts; but even when the passages are parallel, the longer manuscripts tend to be more full and detailed. At the same time there is so much verbal similarity when the passages correspond that a common source must be supposed.

The form of 2 Enoch is what one finds in Jewish Wisdom literature and Jewish Apocalyptic literature. It has been suggested that the longer version is characterized by editorial expansions and Christian interpolations. Hence, the shorter version contains fewer Christian elements. The author of 2 Enoch speaks much of the Creator and final judgment, but he speaks very little, about redemption, which seems to be absent from the thoughts of the author. Indeed, there seems to be a total lack of a Savior or Redeemer in 2 Enoch. What is noteworthy is that 2 Enoch has no reference to the mercy of God.

In the long version presented here, it appears that the last portion of the text was added as an afterthought. It contains the rise of Melchizedek. The appearance of Melchizedek ties 2 Enoch to several other texts forming a Melchizedkian tradition. The author of 2 Enoch follows a tradition in which an aged mother, who had been barren up to her deathbed, miraculously conceived Melchizedek without human intervention. Before she was able to give birth to the baby she died. The baby then emerged from her dead body with the maturity of a three-year-old boy. His priesthood will be perpetuated throughout the generations until "another Melchizedek" appears. If the last Melchizedek serves as the archpriest for the last generation, it indicates that in the mind of this Jewish writer, the Temple was to be rebuilt and would be the place were God would meet His people when the heathen nations were destroyed. The continuation and victory of the Jews as the selected and blessed people of God is implied. In this vein, 2 Enoch follows certain apocalyptic writings.

(For more information on apocalyptic writings see "End of Days" by Joseph Lumpkin.)

The Slavonic version is translated from a Greek source. Most scholars agree that there was either a Hebrew or Aramaic original lying behind the Greek source from which the Slavonic manuscripts were produced. The Hebrew origins are indicated by "Semitisms" in the work, but there are also Greek words and expressions, such as the names of the planets in chapter 30.

Proof that The Slavonic Enoch was written in Greek is shown by the derivation of Adam's name, and by several coincidences with the Septuagint. The origin of the story is perhaps based on Hebrew traditions and certain Semitic turns of language show up in the text. This tends to indicate that there was at one time a Hebrew or Aramaic text that preceded the Greek. From the Greek it was translated into Slavonic. Of this version there are five manuscripts or pieces thereof found.

The short version or the Slavonic Enoch was probably written by a single author in an attempt to bring all the current traditions about Enoch of his time into a central storyline and system. The schema to accomplish the unity of traditions implements Enoch's ascension through multiple heavens. This author was probably a Jew living in Egypt. There are several elements in the book, which betray Egyptian origin. The longer version of 2 Enoch was seeded with Christian elements and appended with an ending that does not fit well, illuminating the fact that there were several authors involved in the longer version.

Parts of the book was probably written in the late first century A.D. The first date is a limit set by the fact that Ethiopic Enoch, Ecclesiasticus, and Wisdom of Solomon are used as sources or references within the text; the second date is a limit set by the fact that the destruction of the Temple is not mentioned at all.

The Slavonic Enoch furnishes new material for the study of religious thought in the beginning of the Common Era. The ideas of the millennium and of the multiple heavens are the most important in this connection. Another very interesting feature is the presence of evil in heaven, the fallen angels in the second heaven, and hell in the third. The idea of evil in heaven may be a nod to the book of Job and the dialog between God and Satan, who was coming and going between heaven and earth. The idea of hell in the third heaven may have been derived from ideas expressed in the

Old Testament book of Isaiah, which mentions that the sufferings of the wicked will be witnessed by the righteous in paradise.

Chapter 21 and forward for several chapters shows a heavy influence of Greek mythology. The Zodiac is mentioned along with heavenly bodies with names such as Zeus, Cronus, Aphrodite, and others. The part of the text containing names and astrological descriptions could have been tampered with as late as the seventh century A.D.

By far, the most interesting and confusing section begins around chapter 25 and runs for several chapters. Here the text takes a turn toward Gnostic theology and cosmology. The Gnostics were a Christian sect, which formed and grew in the first century A.D. and thrived in the second century A.D.

Although Gnostic borrowed from Plato's (428 B.C. – 348 B.C.) creation myth, the maturity and construction of the story shows it to be of Gnostic Christian origin, placing it no earlier than the last part of the first century A.D. and no later than the end of the Second century. Add to the dating question the fact that the destruction of the Temple in Jerusalem is not mentioned, which leads to a date just before

70 A.D., if one assumes the Gnostic flavor was not added later.

The history of the text is obviously long and varied. It probably began as a Jewish oral tradition with pieces taken from several Enochian stories. It was first penned in Hebrew or Aramaic. The date of this incarnation of the text is unknown. Later, the story was expanded and embellished by Greek influences. Lastly, Christians and Gnostics commandeered the book and added their own matter. Thus 2 Enoch exhibits a kaleidoscope of cultural and religious contributions over a great scope of time from the first century B.C. (assuming it came after 1 Enoch) and ending as late as the seventh century A.D. These additions would allow any serious student insight into how ancient texts evolve.

Second Enoch was rediscovered and published in the early 19th century A.D. The text before you uses the R. H. Charles and W. R. Morfill translation of 1896 with additions from other sources. Archaic terms and sentence structure were revised or explained to convey a more modern rendering for the twenty-first century readers.

The Third Book of Enoch

It was not until the early 1900's that The Hebrew Book of Enoch, or 3 Enoch, could be reconstructed. Although the text claims to be written around 100 A.D. it was likely written by a highly educated Rabbi around 300 to 400 A.D. and preserved only in fragments, here and there. Then, in 1928 Dr. Hugo Odeberg PhD. gathered the various Hebrew fragmentary sources and published the first full translation along with copious scholarly notes, including the source Hebrew material. The University Press at Cambridge, in the United Kingdom, published the book. A photocopy of the book made its way to the United State and into the University of Chicago library, where it was kept for many years. It was from this body of work and from this photocopied and preserved manuscript that some of the Hebrew source of this work was compiled. The material was then compared to and supplemented with dozens of other articles and sources to produce this work.

3 Enoch purports to have been written around 100 A.D., but its origins can only be traced to the late fourth or early fifth centuries. Other names for 3 Enoch include "The Third Book of Enoch" and "The Book of the Palaces." The angelology and description of heaven in 1 Enoch is built upon and greatly expanded in 3 Enoch.

The book is rife with Hebrew words, which have no single English equivalent. Even though care was taken to define the majority of these words when first they appear in the text, the reader should expect only keywords to replace or augment meanings thereafter. To do otherwise would either leave the reader to remember the meanings of all Hebrew words or bloat the book to the point of making it difficult to follow.

Modern scholars describe this book as belonging to a body of work called the pseudepigraphia. 3 Enoch claims to be written by a Rabbi, who became a 'high priest' after he had visions of an ascension to Heaven, 90 AD - 135 AD. Rabbi Ishmael is a leading figure of Merkabah literature; however, a number of scholars suggest that it was in fact written by a number of people over a prolonged period of time.

Merkabah writings had to do with the theme of ascension into heaven. The name is derived from a Hebrew word meaning "chariot," referring to Ezekiel's vision beginning in Ezekiel 1:4. Enoch's contents and ideas are unique and newer than those shown in other Merkabah texts, suggesting the book may be among the first in the Merkabah movement or that it is derived through unique influences.

As the other name of this book implies, 3 Enoch is also part of the Temple or Hekalot body of literature. The name Sefer Hekhalot means, "Palaces" or "Temples."

As with 1 Enoch, the exact dating of this book is a difficult task, but some scholars believe it was completed around the time of the Babylonian Talmud, which was around the early 5th century A.D.

3 Enoch was originally written in Hebrew, although it contains a number of words from both Greek and Latin. Parts of the book seem to have been influenced by 1 Enoch, showing the author was familiar with the Mystical Enochian Tradition.

Similar points appearing in 1 Enoch and 3 Enoch are:
    Enoch ascends to Heaven in a storm chariot (3 Enoch 6:1; 7:1)
    Enoch is translated into an angel (3 Enoch 9:1-5; 15:1-2)
    Enoch, as an angel, is given authority in Heaven (3 Enoch 10:1- 3; 16:1)
    Enoch receives an explanation or vision of creation and cosmology. (3 Enoch 13:1-2)
    Enoch sees a hostile angel named Azazel (3 Enoch 4:6; 5:9)

The main theme, throughout the book is the change or "transubstantiation" of Enoch into the angel Metatron.

Metatron appears in various Jewish, Christian, and Islamic works but was a central focus in medieval Jewish mystical texts and occult sources. Rabbinical texts point to Metatron as the angel who stilled the hand of Abraham, preventing him from sacrificing Isaac.

The place and authority of Metatron has been hotly debated, and is seen even within the book. He is seen as sitting in heaven. This is only permitted if one is a deity. He is referred to in the text as

"The Lesser YHWH."

YHWH makes up the Tetragrammaton forming the name we pronounce as "Yahweh" or "Jehovah." The four letters making up the divine name are Yodh, He Waw, He, having the sounds of "Y", "H", "W, O, U or a place holder", and "H." When "He" ends a word it is often silent. Due to the fact that German theologians were heavily involved in theological research and study, one may also find the Tetragrammaton rendered as YHVH, since the V in German has a W sound.

There is a very personal attack within the text, which should be explained. A curse is placed on a man known only as Acher. In Hebrew the name means, "the other," and is used as a term of alienation from the rabbinic community. The Talmud tells us that Elisha be Abuyah entered Paradise in a vision and saw Metatron sitting down (an action that in heaven is permitted only to God himself). Elishah ben Abuyah therefore looked to Metatron as a deity and proclaimed, "There are indeed two powers in heaven!" The other rabbis explain that Metatron was allowed to sit because he was the Heavenly Scribe, writing down the deeds of Israel (Babylonian Talmud, Hagiga 15a).

The intense hatred for any idea hinting at dualism or polytheism, as opposed to monotheism, caused such a reaction within the Rabbinical community that they labeled Elisha be Abuyah a heretic. In 3 Enoch this point is driven home when the entire nation of Israel is to be reconciled to God, except for Acher, whose name is blotted out.

In spite of the disagreements within the ancient Jewsih community, the reader is still left to wonder what position Metatron occupies in heaven. Metatron is described in two ways: as a primordial angel (9:2–13:2) and as the transformation of Enoch after he was assumed into Heaven, and he is called "The Lesser YHWH."

Enoch walked with God; then he was no more, because God took him away. [Genesis 5:24 NIV.]
This Enoch, whose flesh was turned to flame, his veins to fire, his eye-lashes to flashes of lightning, his eye-balls to flaming torches, and whom God placed on a throne next to the throne of glory, received after this heavenly transformation the name Metatron. [3 Enoch]

As the Christian community came in contact with the Jewish book of 3 Enoch, they had little trouble reconciling the names and position of Metatron. To those Christians a person who may sit in heaven and who judges, and who is called by the same name taken by God must be Yeshua (Jesus.)

It may be of help if the meaning of the name, Metatron, could be ascertained, but it is not clear. Suggestions are that the name originated from the root words of such phrases as, "keeper of the watch," "guard," "to protect," "one who serves behind the throne," "one who occupies the throne next to the throne of glory," "to lead," or " to measure." None of these suggestions can be proven. From the text itself we know only that Metatron is referred to as "the youth," likely because he would be the newest and youngest angel. He is also called, "the prince of the presence (of God)." His purpose in heaven was to be a witness against mankind.

A type of numerology is used and referred to within the text. Temurah is one of the three ancient methods used by Cabbalist to rearrange words and sentences in the Torah, in the belief that by this method they can derive the deeper, hidden spiritual meaning of the words. Temurah may be used to change letters in certain words to create a new meaning for a Biblical statement. Another method is called Gematria. In this method letters are substituted for numbers and the meaning of words with the same value are compared along with the numerical meaning of the words.

A preparatory summery of the first section of the book may be framed as a revelation from Metatron, or the Prince of the Presence, to Rabbi Ishmael. Metatron, as it turns out, is Enoch and this is why the title of this book has come to be called, "3 Enoch." Any question as to who Metatron may be is answered clearly in CHAPTER 4, where it is written, "Rabbi Ishmael said: I asked Metatron and said to him: " why are you called by the name of your Creator, by seventy names? You are greater than all the princes, higher than all the angels, beloved more than all the servants, honored above all the mighty ones in kingship, greatness and glory: why do they call you 'Youth' in the high heavens?" He answered and said to me: "Because I am Enoch, the son of Jared. For when the generation of the flood sinned and were confounded in their deeds, saying unto God: Depart from us, for we desire not the knowledge of your ways (Job 21:14), then the Holy One, blessed be He, removed me from their midst to be a witness against them in the high heavens to all the inhabitants of the world, that they may not say: 'The Merciful One is cruel'.

The following text begins the book of 3 Enoch. Notes and explanations are italicized. Words placed in parentheses are alternate renderings of a word or phrase.

The Book of Jubilees

The Book of Jubilees, also known as The Little Genesis and The Apocalypse of Moses, opens with an extraordinary claim of authorship. It is attributed to the very hand of Moses; penned while he was on Mount Sinai, as an angel of God dictated to him regarding those events that transpired from the beginning of the world. The story is written from the viewpoint of the angel.

The angelic monolog takes place after the exodus of the children of Israel out of Egypt. The setting is atop Mount Sinai, where Moses was summoned by God. The text then unfolds as the angel reveals heaven's viewpoint of history. We are led through the creation of man, Adam's fall from grace, the union of fallen angels and earthly women, the birth of demonic offspring, the cleansing of the earth by flood, and the astonishing claim that man's very nature was somehow changed, bringing about a man with less sinful qualities than his antediluvian counterpart.

The story goes on to fill in many details in Israel's history, ending at the point in time when the narrative itself takes place, after the exodus.

Scholars believe Jubilees was composed in the second century B.C. The Hebrew fragments found at Qumran are part of a Jewish library that contained other supporting literature such as the Book of Enoch and others.

An analysis of the chronological development in the shapes of letters in the manuscripts confirms that Jubilees is pre-Christian in date and seems to have been penned between 100 and 200 B.C. The book of Jubilees is also cited in the Qumran Damascus Document in pre-Christian texts.

The author was a Pharisee (a doctor of the law), or someone very familiar with scripture and religious law. Since the scrolls were found in what is assumed to be an Essene library, and were dated to the time the Essene community was active, the author was probably a member of that particular religious group. Jubilees represents a hyper-legalistic and midrashic tendency, which was part of the Essene culture at the time.

Jubilees represents a midrash on Genesis 1:1 through Exodus 12 depicting the episodes from creation with the observance of the

Sabbath by the angels and men; to Israel's escape from Egyptian bondage.

Although originally written in Hebrew, the Hebrew texts were completely lost until the find at Qumran. Fragments of Jubilees were discovered among the Dead Sea Scrolls. At least fourteen copies of the Book of Jubilees have been identified from caves 1, 2, 3 and 11 at Qumran. This makes it clear that the Book of Jubilees was a popular and probably authoritative text for the community whose library was concealed in the caves. These fragments are actually generations closer to the original copies than most books in our accepted Bible. Unfortunately, the fragments found at Qumran were only pieces of the texts and offered the briefest of glimpses of the entire book. The only complete versions of the Book of Jubilees are in Ethiopic, which in turn were translations of a Greek version.

Four Ethiopian manuscripts of Jubilees were found to be hundreds of years old. Of these, the fifteenth and sixteenth century texts are the truest and least corrupted when compared to the fragments found at Qumran. There are also citations of Jubilees in Syriac literature that may reflect a lost translation from Hebrew. Pieces of Latin translations have also been found.

Other fragments of a Greek version are quoted or referenced by Justin Martyr, Origen, Diodorus of Antioch, Isidore of Alexandria, Isidore of Seville, Eutychius, Patriarch of Alexandria, John of Malala, and Syncellus. This amount of varied information and translations is enough to allow us to reconstruct the original to a great degree. The internal evidence of Jubilees shows very little tampering by Christians during its subsequent translations, allowing a clear view of certain Jewish beliefs propagated at the time of its origin. By removing certain variances, we can isolate Christian alterations and mistakes in translations with a reasonable degree of confidence. Due to the poor condition of the fragments of Qumran, we may never be able to confirm certain key phrases in Hebrew. Thus, as with many texts, including the Bible, in the end we must trust in the accuracy of the ancient translators.

It should be noted that the books of Jubilees, Enoch, and Jasher present stories of "The Watchers," a group of angels sent to earth to record and teach, but who fell by their own lust and pride into a demonic state. Both Enoch and Jubilees refer to a solar-based calendar. This may show a conflict or transition at the time of their penning since Judaism now uses a lunar-based calendar.

Laws, rites, and functions are observed and noted in Jubilees. Circumcision is emphasized in both humans and angels. Angelic observance of Sabbath laws as well as parts of Jewish religious laws are said to have been observed in heaven before they were revealed to Moses.

To the Qumran community, complete obedience to the Laws of Moses entailed observing a series of holy days and festivals at a particular time according to a specific calendar. The calendar described in Jubilees is one of 364 days, divided into four seasons of three months each with thirteen weeks to a season. Each month had 30 days with one day added at certain times for each of the four seasons. With 52 weeks in a year, the festival and holy days recur at the same point each year. This calendar became a hallmark of an orthodox Qumran community.

The adherence to a specific calendar is one of many ways the Book of Jubilees shows the devotion to religious law. The law had been placed at the pinnacle of importance in the lives of the community at Qumran. All aspects of life were driven by a seemingly obsessive compliance to every jot and tittle of the law. The Book Of Jubilees confirms what can only be inferred from the books of Ezra, Nehemiah, and Zechariah, that the law and those who carried it out were supreme.

As the law took hold, by its nature, it crystallized the society. Free expression died, smothered under a mantle of hyper-orthodoxy. Since free thought invited accusations of violations of the law or claims of heresy, prudence, a closed mind, and a silent voice prevailed. Free thought was limited to religious or apocryphal writings, which upheld the orthodox positions of the day. The silent period between Malachi and Mark may be a reflection of this stasis. Jubilees, Enoch, and other apocryphal books found in the Qumran caves are a triumph over the unimaginative mindset brought on by making religious law supreme and human expression contrary to the law and punishable by death. It may be an odd manifestation that such a burst of creativity was fueled by the very search for order that suppressed free thought in the first place.

The Book of Jubilees seems to be an attempt to answer and explain all questions left unanswered in the Book of Genesis as well as to bolster the position of the religious law. It attempts to

trace the source of religious laws back to an ancient beginning
thereby adding weight and sanction.

In the Book of Jubilees, we discover the origin of the wife of
Cain. There is information offered about angels and the
beginnings of the human race, how demons came into existence,
and the place of Satan in the plans of God. Information is offered
in an attempt to make perfect sense of the vagaries left in Genesis.
For the defense of order and law and to maintain religious law as
the center point of Jewish life, Jubilees was written as an answer to
both pagan Greeks and liberal Jews. From the divine placement
of law and order to its explanation of times and events, Jubilees is
a panorama of legalism.

The name "Jubilees" comes from the division of time into eras
known as Jubilees. One Jubilee occurs after the equivalent of forty-
nine years, or seven Sabbaths of weeks of years have passed. It is
the numerical perfection of seven sevens. In a balance and
symmetry of years, the Jubilee occurs after seven cycles of seven
or forty-nine years have been completed. Thus, the fiftieth year is
a Jubilee year. Time is told by referencing the number of Jubilees
that have transpired from the time the festival was first kept. For
example, Israel entered Canaan at the close of the fiftieth jubilee,
which is about 2450 B.C.

The obsession with time, dates, and the strict observance of
festivals are all evidence of legalism taken to the highest level.

Based on the approximate time of writing, Jubilees was
created in the time of the Maccabees, in the high priesthood of
Hyrcanus. In this period of time the appearance of the Messiah

and the rise of the Messianic kingdom were viewed as imminent. Followers were preparing themselves for the arrival of the Messiah and the establishment of His eternal kingdom.

Judaism was in contact with the Greek culture at the time. The Greeks were known to be philosophers and were developing processes of critical thinking. One objective of Jubilees was to defend Judaism against the attacks of the Hellenists and to prove that the law was logical, consistent, and valid. Attacks against paganism and non-believers are embedded in the text along with defense of the law and its consistency through proclamations of the law being observed by the angels in heaven from the beginning of creation.

Moral lessons are taught by use of the juxtaposition of the "satans" and their attempts to test and lead mankind into sin against the warning and advice of scriptural wisdom from Moses and his angels.

Mastema is mentioned only in The Book of Jubilees and in the Fragments of a Zadokite Work. Mastema is Satan. The name Mastema is derived from the Hebrew, "Mastim," meaning "adversary." The word occurs as singular and plural. The word is equivalent to Satan (adversary or accuser). This is similar to the chief Satan and his class of "satans" in 1 Enoch 40,7.

Mastema is subservient to God. His task is to tempt men to sin and if they do, he accuses them in the presence of the Throne of God. He and his minions lead men into sin but do not cause the sin. Once men have chosen to sin, they lead them from sin to destruction. Since man is given free will, sin is a choice, with

Mastema simply encouraging and facilitating the decision. The choice, we can assume, is our own and the destruction that follows is "self-destruction."

Beliar is also mentioned. Beliar is the Greek name for Belial / Beliaal. The name in its Hebrew equivalent means "without value." This was a demon known by the Jews as the chief of all the devils. Belial is the leader of the Sons of Darkness. Belial and Mastema are mentioned in a Zadokite fragment saying that at the time of the Antichrist, Belial shall be let loose against Israel; as God spoke through Isaiah the prophet. Belial is sometimes presented as an agent of God's punishment although he is considered a "Satan."

It is important to mention that Judaism had no doctrine of original sin. The fall of Adam and Eve may have removed man from the perfect environment and the curses that followed may have shortened his lifespan, but propagation of sin through the bloodline was not considered. Sin seemed to affect only man and the animals he was given dominion over. Yet man continued to sin, and to increase in his capacity and modes of sin. The explanation offered for man's inability to resist is the existence of fallen angels; spiritual, superhuman creatures whose task it was to teach us but who now tempted and misled men. In the end, the world declines and crumbles under the evil influence of the fallen angels turned demons called, "The Watchers."

With the establishment of the covenant between Abraham and God, we are told that God had appointed spirits to "mislead" all the nations but would not assign a spirit to lead or mislead the children of Isaac as God himself would be leading them.

The angels converse in Hebrew as it is the heavenly tongue. The law is written by God using this alphabet thus the law is also holy. All men spoke Hebrew until the time of Babel when the Hebrew language was lost. However, when Abraham dedicated himself to God, his ears were opened and his tongue was sanctified and Hebrew was again spoken and understood.

Finally, the entire text is based on the numbers of forty-nine and fifty. Forty-nine represents the pinnacle of perfection, being made up of seven times seven. The number fifty, which is the number of the Jubilee, is the number of grace. In the year of Jubilee slaves were to be set free, debts were forgiven, and grace filled the land and people.

Drawing from the theology and myths at the time, the Book of Jubilees expands and embellishes on the creation story, the fall of Adam and Eve, and the fall of the angels. The expanded detail written into the text may have been one reason it was eventually rejected. However, the effects of the book can still be seen throughout the Judeo-Christian beliefs of today. The theology espoused in Jubilees can be seen in the angelology and demonology taught in the Christian churches of today and widely held by many Jews.

In an attempt to answer questions left unaddressed in Genesis the writer confronts the origin and identification of Cain's wife. According to the Book Of Jubilees, Cain married his sister, as did all of the sons of Adam and Eve, except Abel, who was murdered. This seemed offensive to some, since it flies in the face of the very law it was written to defend. Yet this seemed to the writer to be the lesser of evils, given the problematic questions. Inbreeding was dismissed with the observation that the law was not fully given and understood then. The effects of the act were moot due to the purity of the newly created race.

The seeming discrepancy between the divine command of Adam's death decree and the timing of his death is addressed. Seeing that Adam continued to live even after he ate the fruit, which was supposed to bring on his death, the writer set about to clarify God's actions. The problem is explained away is a single sentence. Since a day in heaven is as a thousand years on earth and Adam died having lived less than a thousand years this meant he died in the same heavenly day. Dying within the same day of the crime was acceptable.

In an astonishing parallel to the Book of Enoch, written at about the same time as Jubilees, the Watchers, or sons of God mentioned in Genesis 6, fell from grace when they descended to earth and had sex with the daughters of men. In the Book of Enoch, the angels descended for the purpose of seducing the women of earth.

However, in The Book of Jubilees, the angels were sent to teach men, but after living on earth for a while, they were tempted by their own lust and fell from heaven. The offspring of this unholy union were bloodthirsty and cannibalistic giants.

The Book of Jubilees indicates that each of the offspring was somehow different. Because of this, they are divided into categories of the Nephilim (or Naphidim, depending on the transliteration), the Giants, and the Eljo. The Nephil are mentioned however this word is the singular of Nephilim. Therefore, we have these classifications or species living on the earth: Angels, also referred to as watchers; Nephilim; Eljo; Giants; and Human.

The Nephilim seem to be a being that contains an evil spirit much like their fathers. The giants, although coming from the same union of angel and woman, were carnal creatures. We have little information about the Eljo except they lived to kill men. They could be the "men of renown" mentioned in the Bible. These may have been the beings that brought about the myths of the violent and angry creatures such as the Cyclops or gods of war.

As sin spread throughout the world and the minds of men were turned toward evil, God saw no alternative but to cleanse the earth with a flood and establish a "new nature" in man that does not have to sin. It is this new nature that the Messiah will meet in mankind when He comes. As far as this author is aware, the re-creation of man's nature is mentioned in no other book. This idea of human nature being altered as it existed before the flood is found nowhere else but in Jubilees.

The angelic narrator tells us there were times in Israel's history when no evil existed and all men lived in accord. We are also told when and where the satans were allowed to attack and confound Israel. In this narrative, God uses his satans to harden the hearts of the Egyptians so they pursued Israel and were destroyed.

"The Apocalypse of Moses" also denotes the same work. This

title seems to have been used for only a short period of time. It refers to the revelation given to Moses as the recipient of all the knowledge disclosed in the book. The term "Apocalypse" means to make known or to reveal. Another title of Jubilees is "Little Genesis". This refers to the lesser, non-canon status of the book. With the exception of minor differences picked up through translation and copying, the three titles represent the same text.

The Book of Genesis

Genesis is the first book of the Old Testament in both the Jewish and Christian Bibles. Genesis means the act or process of producing, thus the text is named for the creation story.

The first eleven chapters are adapted from Mesopotamian and Canaanite traditions regarding the creation of earth. Other story lines were added to account for the existence of man by incorporating stories about Adam and Eve. The story of the flood is brought into Genesis, although it is difficult to know exactly which region the story was taken from as practically every culture has such a story. It is generally assumed the Deluge story was acquired from the same culture the creation story element was taken.

Although traditionally The Book of Genesis is attributed to Moses, most modern scholars agree that the book is a composite of at least three different literary strands: J (10th century B.C.), E (9th century), and P (5th century). Oddly, one of the contributors seems to have a "feminine" voice and could have been penned, or at least influenced by a woman.

At the time of the "J" document, a despot ruled over the Jews around 560 B.C. The writer of "J" may have written the book to document the people's oral history and thus give them hope and ensure there would be a record of their connection to their God, fearing their destruction.

Since three stories were being interwoven, the writer of Genesis took the J,P, and E stories and combined them, removing parts that were contrary to the religious beliefs of the day. One set of writings used the Canaanite term, "Elohim," as the name of the creator God. A second used the more ancient Judean word transliterated from Hebrew and rendered "Jehovah" in English, to describe its God.

By removing inconsistencies and repetitions a smooth storyline emerged. The story coming from the Canaanite culture contained polytheistic beliefs. Traces of the two different gods and their differing personalities, as well as the Canaanite belief in polytheism may remain, but since the Jews had come to embrace monotheism at that time, the writer attempted to remove traces of such variances.

For a more complete picture it is always best to keep all stories and books in context. The complete translations of the non-biblical books used in this work can be obtained in "The Lost Books of the Bible: The Great Rejected Texts" by Joseph Lumpkin, published by Fifth Estate.

The Lost Books of the Bible: The Great Rejected Texts

The Lost Books of the Bible: The Great Rejected Texts -

Eighteen of the most sought after books available, which shed light on the evolution of our faith, our theology, and our church. Translations and commentary by the author of the best selling book, "The Lost Book of Enoch," Joseph B. Lumpkin.
- Section One: Lost Scriptures of the Old Testament- First Book of Adam and Eve, Second Book of Adam and Eve, First Book of Enoch, Second Book of Enoch (Secrets of Enoch), Jubilees, Jasher, The Story of Ahikar
- Section Two: Apocalyptic Writings and the End of Days- Apocalypse of Abraham, Apocalypse of Thomas 4 Ezra, 2 Baruch, War Scroll (Sons of Dark vs. Sons of Light)
- Section Three: Lost Scriptures of the New Testament- Gospel of Philip, Gospel of Mary Magdalene, Apocryphon of John, Gospel of Thomas, Gospel of Judas, Acts Chapter 29

Book of the Giants

The Book of the Giants is found in fragments only and was part of the cache' of the Dead Sea documents. It tells the story of the 200 fallen angels and their dreams and fears after their fall. Enoch lived before the Flood, during a time when the world was very different and angels and humans interacted freely. This fact is neutrally reported in Genesis (6:1-4), but other stories view this episode as the source of the corruption that made the punishing flood necessary. According to The Book of Enoch, the mingling of angel and human was actually the idea of Shernihaza, the leader of the evil angels, who lured 200 others to cohabit with women. The offspring of these unnatural unions were giants. The wicked angels and the giants began to oppress the human population and to teach them to do evil. For this reason God determined to imprison the angels until the final judgment and to destroy the earth with a flood. Enoch's efforts to intercede with heaven for the fallen angels were unsuccessful (1 Enoch 6-16).

The Book of Giants retells part of this story and elaborates on the exploits of the giants, especially the two children of Shemihaza, Ohya and Hahya. Since no complete manuscript exists of Giants, its exact contents and their order remain a matter of guesswork. Most of the content of the present fragments concerns the giants' ominous dreams and Enoch's efforts to interpret them and to intercede with God on the giants' behalf. Unfortunately, little remains of the independent adventures of the giants, but it is likely that these tales were at least partially derived from ancient Near Eastern mythology. Thus the name of one of the giants is Gilgamesh, the Babylonian hero and subject of a great epic written in the third millennium B.C.E.

The Apocryphon of John

The Apocryphon, or "Secrets" of John forms the cornerstone of Gnostic mythology and cosmology. In this text we are introduced to the major entities of creation and lordship. We learn how the universe, including earth and man, came into being. The origin of evil, the creator god, and the material world are explained in detail. The story seems to be a mixture of various belief systems, including Chrithat of Plato, who seems to have borrowed freely from the format of Greek mythology, and Christianity. The story is loosely based on Genesis chapters 1 through 13 as a timeline.

The basic text of the Apocryphon of John existed in some form before 185 A.D. when a book called the Apocryphon of John was referred to by Irenaeus in his book, Against Heresies (Adversus Haereses), written in that year. Part of the mythology revealed in the Apocryphon of Jonh is also present in the Gnostic book, The Sophia (Wisdom) of Jesus as well as other Gnostic texts.

The document that so angered Irenaeus was lost and remained so until 1945, when a library of papyrus codices from the 4th century were found at Nag Hammadi in Egypt. The Apocryphon of John was among the texts.

Even though the codices were dated from c. A.D. 300 – A.D. 400 they were all copies of texts that existed in various forms long before then.

www.ingramcontent.com/pod-product-compliance
Lightning Source LLC
Chambersburg PA
CBHW052042090426
42739CB00010B/2015